GARLAND STUDIES IN

THE HISTORY OF AMERICAN LABOR

edited by

STUART BRUCHEY
UNIVERSITY OF MAINE

A GARLAND SERIES

THE IMPACT OF TRADE ON UNITED STATES EMPLOYMENT

CATHERINE SVEIKAUSKAS

GARLAND PUBLISHING, Inc.
New York & London / 1995

Library of Congress Cataloging-in-Publication Data

Sveikauskas, Catherine, 1947–
    The impact of trade on United States employment / Catherine
Sveikauskas.
        p.   cm. — (Garland studies in the history of American
labor)
    Includes bibliographical references and index.
    ISBN 0-8153-2306-9 (alk. paper)
    1. Foreign trade and employment—United States. 2. Foreign
trade and employment—United States—Econometric models. I.
Title. II. Series.
HD5710.75.U6S87 1995
331.12'0973—dc20   95-25934

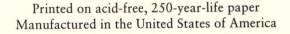

Printed on acid-free, 250-year-life paper
Manufactured in the United States of America

For Chris and Andrew, who will come of age in the 21st Century

Contents

Tables

Preface

Over the last several years there has been much concern that international trade has been destroying "good" jobs in the United States. This book provides a thorough empirical examination of this issue, focussing on the years when large, continuous deficits began.

Good jobs are defined in terms of the earnings of full-time workers in each education group. Consequently, different occupations can provide "good" jobs for workers with an elementary schoool education, some high school, high school graduates, some college, college graduates, and workers with a post-graduate education.

The effect of international trade on employment in each occupation is determined through the Leamer-Bowen methodology, which examines the effect of net trade on occupational employment through a standard input-output methodology, and compares the trade influence with that of domestic consumption.

The analysis examines occupational employment data for 118 occupations in 156 different industries. The input-output table is for 1977. Net exports are studied for 1977, 1982, and 1985, a time period which spans the beginnings of very large trade deficits. Occupational earnings in each education category are obtained from the 1980 *Census of Population*.

The results indicate that from 1977 to 1982, when the trade deficit was roughly stable, international trade provided good jobs for workers in every educational group. However, from 1982 to 1985, when the trade deficit increased sharply, international trade destroyed good jobs for high school dropouts and high school graduates, two groups for whom labor market concern is often expressed.

The cross-section evidence also varies. Trade did not create good jobs in 1977, strongly created good jobs in 1982, but no longer did so in 1985, except for the highly educated.

The deficits of the early 1980's peaked in 1987, declined for several years, and now are rising strongly again. They will increase more if the dollar strengthens. On balance, over the period studied in this book, trade created relatively good jobs, but conclusions differ with the particular year examined.

xi

Acknowledgments

I would like to thank John Tschetter, formerly of the Office of Economic Growth of the Bureau of Labor Statistics, for compressing the Economic Growth Project occupation by industry matrices to the 134 occupation categories used here. This book could not have been written without John's help in classifying the occupations and compressing the massive data base to manageable size. I thank Karen Horowitz, also of the Economic Growth Project, for providing me with the detailed 156-sector Economic Growth Project input-output table for 1977, and Kevin Delaney of the Office of Productivity and Technology at BLS for his expert help in advising me how to get these massive data sets on diskettes, so that I could use them on my personal computer.

I also thank Leo Sveikauskas for patiently explaining the detailed methodology used in his 1983 article, and for carefully helping me find the errors in the computer programs on the many occasions when they did not work and it was not clear why. Thanks are due to my brother, Anthony Defina, who installed my home computer, especially the additional memory and the math coprocessor necessary for the earlier calculations for this book. For the final draft, I must thank my sons, Chris and Andrew, who installed the word processing software necessary for the page layout. Very special thanks are also due to Penny Mayorga, my friend and neighbor, whose guidance was crucial to formatting this book.

Finally, I would like to thank Professor Christopher Clague, at the University of Maryland, chairman of the dissertation committee upon which this book is based, for many conversations in which the topic and methodology gradually evolved to its present form. I am also most grateful to Professors Katherine Abraham and Marie Howland for many constructive and helpful comments.

The Impact of Trade on United States Employment

I

Introduction and Theory

INTRODUCTION

In 1986, Thurow (1986) suggested that international trade was now systematically destroying high-wage jobs in the United States. However, he presented no empirical evidence for this conjecture. This book conducts comprehensive empirical tests examining whether international trade is, in fact, currently destroying the best American jobs. It is well-known (Baldwin (1971), L. Sveikauskas (1983)) that the United States exports goods produced by high-wage labor with professional or managerial skills and imports goods produced by blue-collar skills such as operatives and laborers. From this perspective, it is clear that, on balance, trade provides Americans with good jobs and eliminates relatively unskilled positions.

The present book extends beyond prior work in the following three respects:

First, this book considers 118 separate occupational categories, which provides far more detail than the nine or ten major occupational groups considered in earlier studies.

Second, this book compares the impact of trade on American jobs in 1982-1985, when the trade deficit reached unprecedented levels, with the impact of the much smaller deficits which occurred in earlier years. In particular, was the effect of trade on jobs in 1982-1985 different from the effect in earlier years, or were the effects much the same?

Third, occupational distributions may not fully describe how good certain American jobs are, as in the case of a steel industry operative who is very highly paid. This book therefore also uses information on earnings in each occupation, the education in each occupation, and the earnings paid to different education groups within each occupation to determine whether "good" American jobs are currently being lost to foreign trade.

Moreover, this book adopts the Leamer-Bowen theoretical methodology to assess the impact of trade on the labor force, a methodology newly emerging in the international trade literature to calculate the factor content of international trade. This methodology has advantages over the regression technique for this purpose.[1] The main advantage of the Leamer-Bowen methodology is that it directly indicates the export of factor services. Proponents of the regression method may believe that the regression coefficients will reflect net factor exports, but it is uncertain whether this is the case.

In this book, the effect of trade on each of 118 occupational categories is examined by treating each of these occupations as a separate factor input. Following the theoretical framework of Leamer (1980), the effect of trade on each factor is examined by calculating the net exports of each factor embodied in total trade. The amount of each of these factors embodied in trade is calculated from input-output tables and includes both direct and indirect input requirements. Following Bowen (1983), net exports are normalized by national consumption of each factor, which allows the effect of trade on each type of labor to be expressed in percentage terms.

The skill content of net exports, derived from this new and preferred methodology in the international trade literature, is then econometrically analyzed in terms of education and earnings, variables widely accepted in the labor economics literature as simple, direct, and unambiguous measures of human capital. This book combines these central themes from the international trade and labor economics literature to provide conclusive empirical evidence on whether and to what extent the United States is losing "good" jobs to international trade.

The main findings are as follows. First, on a net basis, trade contributed 77,000 jobs in 1977 and 486,000 in 1982, but a loss of 2.5 million jobs in 1985. Thus, on a net basis trade cost the economy 3 million jobs between 1982 to 1985.

Second, over the 1977 to 1982 period, trade, on balance, created good jobs for American workers within every educational category. However, from 1982 to 1985, as the trade deficit deepened, trade destroyed good jobs for U.S. workers in some educational categories, particularly high school dropouts and high school graduates, two groups for whom concern over labor market success is often expressed.

This assessment must be tempered by the cross-section results. Trade certainly created good jobs on balance in 1982, and no longer created good jobs in 1985, but in 1977, the effect of trade was neutral, not positive as one might expect in a period of relatively free trade and modest deficits.

Finally, the finer occupational detail which characterizes this book makes a difference. The findings cited above hold only for the 118 occupational analysis. When analysis is conducted at the level of major occupational groups, which is how all previous studies have approached the relationship between trade and labor quality, no such distinct patterns emerge. Hence, the greater detail at the heart of this book provides a more reliable view of the relationship between trade and good jobs than any previous work.

THEORETICAL STRUCTURE: INTERNATIONAL TRADE

The effect of trade on employment is calculated following Leamer (1980), as:

$$AT = \text{Net trade effect} \qquad (1)$$

in which A is an m x n matrix showing the total input requirements of each of the 118 input factors (m inputs) in each of the 156 (n) industries. A is multiplied by T, an n x 1 vector of net exports of gross output from each of the n industries. The result, which shows the total effects from these multiplications, is an m x 1 matrix showing net exports (or, if negative, net imports) of each of the m inputs. This is the most direct way to compute the net trade in factor services.

Following Bowen (1983), each of these net exports is normalized by national consumption of each of these factors, which is the amount of each factor (both direct and indirect) used in producing the final national demand for each output. Formally, this is calculated as:

$$AC = \text{Consumption} \qquad (2)$$

in which C is an n x 1 matrix showing gross output of each of the commodities supplied to final demand by each industry. Dividing each term in (1) by its counterpart in (2):

$$\text{Relative effect of trade} = \frac{\text{Net trade effect}}{\text{Consumption}} = \frac{AT}{AC} \qquad (3)$$

The effect of trade is determined from the amounts of each factor embodied in trade rather than from the more traditional approach (Baldwin (1971)) of inter-industry regression analysis in which net exports are regressed on factor intensities.

The effect of trade on the occupational distribution is determined by calculating (3) for each of the 118 occupational categories in a given year. For example, in a given year the expression in (3), which we shall call R, may vary from .05 for engineers or .04 for farmers to .03 for glaziers or -.13 for oil field workers.

Values of R can be calculated for the same set of occupations in each year. The value of R will be calculated for each occupation in each year for 1977, 1982, and 1985. (As discussed later, the same input-output table and occupational requirements, and therefore the same A, will be assumed for each year. Only trade, T, and consumption, C, will be allowed to change from year to year. The years were chosen to span the different magnitudes of the trade deficit. An additional consideration was that consumption data are only available on a consistent industry basis for these years.)

Another important area of exploration is the effect of trade on the absolute number of job losses, as given by equation (1). Most previous studies of the effect of trade on the structure of employment have concentrated on the nine or ten major occupational groups. (See, for example, Stone and Sawhill (1986).) This book differs from previous work on the absolute number of job losses in two main ways. First, we will concentrate on the recent 1982-1985 period, in which the trade deficit has been unusually large, and compare these job losses with the amount and pattern of job losses in previous years. Second, this study is conducted in far greater occupational detail than previous work. Such detailed analysis will determine whether trade displacement is a much more severe problem than the data for just the major occupational groups indicate. For example, Sawhill and Stone found trade responsible for a total of 2 million job losses in 1979-84, but their categories included only seven occupational groups, so that job losses within major occupational categories may have been canceled out by job gains within these broad groupings. This book finds that job losses in 1977 and 1982 were about 28 percent higher when the detailed occupations are analyzed than when changes for the 13 occupational groups are considered. However, in 1985 total job losses were not substantially greater when the detailed categories were used instead of the major occupational groups. With the data developed in this book, it will also be possible to address for the first time the related question of whether there are differences in the influence of trade on different occupations within a broad overall major occupational category.

The effect of trade on the number and types of jobs will be examined from equation (1). Implied changes in the distribution of factor abundance from 1982 to 1985 can be stated as $R_{1985}-R_{1982}$ for each of the 118 occupational categories, and for 13 major occupational groups. These changes can then be examined in terms of labor market characteristics within each of these occupational categories.

THEORETICAL STRUCTURE: LABOR MARKET CHARACTERISTICS OF OCCUPATIONS

This book uses two criteria to evaluate a "good" job: earnings and earnings given education. Obviously, the most important characteristic of occupations is the earnings they generate. Therefore, the first key variable used to describe occupations is the mean earnings of full-time workers in each occupation.

The second dimension considered is the mean earnings of workers in each occupational group, given the worker's education. An occupation which pays high wages to individuals with relatively poor educations is a particularly important source of good jobs because these individuals are paid more than they could be paid elsewhere. This variable is computed by comparing mean earnings for workers in each educational class within a particular occupation with mean earnings in each educational class for all workers in general. Thus, we shall examine whether a given occupation is especially "good" for particular education groups, in the sense that it pays workers with a given education especially well compared to all workers in the economy with the same education.

The key characteristics of each occupation are therefore the mean hourly earnings of full-time workers and the mean hourly earnings of full-time workers, given education.

A higher rating in each of these central occupational characteristics is taken as an indication of a "good" job; conversely, lower ratings signify evidence of less acceptable jobs.

The first sequence of tests examines the relationships:

$$R_{1977} = a + bx_i, \ = 1,2,3$$

in which the x's are the earnings in each occupation for a given education level relative to the earnings of all workers with that education level, by simple regression analyses across the 118 different occupational categories. These relationships are examined for each of the years 1977, 1982, and 1985.

Changes in the regression coefficients over time will summarize changes in the structure of trade over time. The study period will be broken into two sub-periods: 1977 to 1982 and 1982 to 1985.

Changes in R over these two periods will be the dependent variable in regressions of the form:

$$R_{1977\text{-}1982}=a+bx_i; \quad R_{1982\text{-}1985}=a+bx_i$$

This sequence of tests will be performed aggregating the 118 occupations to 13 broad occupational groups and results will be compared with results from the 118 occupational level of detail. These regressions will be for all full-time workers; separate regressions will be performed for men only.

EMPIRICAL STUDIES OF THE FACTOR CONTENT OF TRADE

The practice of incorporating skill differences into the analysis of international trade has a long history. The Ohlin model explained international trade in terms of factor endowments. A country exports products intensive in its abundant resource and imports those intensive in its scarce resource. However, Leontief (1956) found that an average million dollars' worth of exports embodies much less capital and slightly less labor than would be required to replace [from domestic production] an equivalent amount of imports. Hence, he concluded that the United States specializes in labor-intensive production. It is well-known that this country had a higher capital-labor ratio than its trading partners; hence, this finding came to be known as the "Leontief paradox."

This paradox spawned an extensive literature offering explanations of this phenomenon. Leontief himself emphasized the superiority of U.S. labor as an explanation. However, Kreinin (1965) surveyed international managers concerning relative worker productivity and found observed labor quality differences were much smaller than required to generate the Leontief results.

Many other researchers explained the paradox more formally by dividing the amorphous category "labor" into skill groups and proceeding empirically. Leontief (1956) originally considered five different classes of labor. Harkness and Kyle (1975) looked at four distinct categories: (1) scientists and engineers; (2) other high skill workers; (3) middle skilled workers; (4) low skilled workers. Keesing (1965) attempted to explain trade flows by breaking labor into five occupational groups: (1) Professional, technical, and clerical;(2) craftsmen and foremen (skilled manual workers); (3) clerical, sales, and service; (4) operatives (semi-skilled); and (5) laborers (unskilled).

Maskus (1985) used engineers and scientists, production labor, and other labor. Baldwin (1971) and Sveikauskas (1983) each used ten or more occupational categories.

This book builds on that work in the sense that it contains much finer occupational detail than any previous study, which makes it possible to conduct comprehensive econometric tests of whether United States is exporting the services of many alternative facets of skilled labor.

This long line of research has established that the United States labor force exports goods produced by highly skilled workers and imports goods which require a lower level of occupational skills (Baldwin (1971), Keesing (1967) and Sveikauskas (1983)). However, no previous study has considered a sufficient number of occupations to reliably establish the econometric relationship between trade and the skills and education of the work force.

Baldwin (1971) regressed net exports against the percentage of the labor force in seven skill groups. He found a significant positive relationship between the percentage of engineers and scientists, and craftsmen and foremen in an industry and the U.S. share of total world exports of that industry. The percentage of operatives and non-farm laborers had negative signs, but were not significant. Coefficients for clerical and sales workers were mildly positive but also not significant. Baldwin's trade data were limited to 1962, his skills data 1958, and he used the regression methodology.

In work examining the role of technology in U.S. foreign trade, L. Sveikauskas (1983) investigated the factor abundance of nine skill groups. Using the same Leamer-Bowen methodology employed here, he found the U.S. to have net exports of professional scientific labor services as well as those of technical managers and somewhat lesser exports of the services of other professionals and managers, sales and clerical workers and craftsmen. Operatives and laborers' skills were, on balance, imported; farm skills exported.

The present book examines 118 occupations instead of seven or nine, a nine-year time span instead of just one, and includes data on services instead of assuming these values are zero. Therefore, this book represents a very considerable improvement over prior work in these directions.

The previous research cited above, and the method adopted in this book, measures the effect of trade on the labor force in terms of the occupational distribution of the labor force. Previous trade researchers have also measured the labor quality content of international trade by the capitalized value of worker wages (Kenen (1965), Balassa (1977), Branson and Monoyios (1977)). This method, first used by Kenen and

Griliches and followed by many trade researchers since then, attributes to human capital the discounted excess of the wage earned in an industry beyond that paid to a man with eight years of education, or unimproved labor. Typically, human capital in each industry is estimated as follows:

$$HK_k = (w_k-w)/0.10 *L_k$$

where HK_k is the level of human capital in industry k, w_k is the average wage in industry k, w is the median wage earned in that year by a male with eight years of education, and L_k is the employment in industry k. The discount rate, 10 percent here, is allowed to vary.

Human capital measured in this way is then either entered as a separate independent variable in a regression which also includes as independent variables physical capital and raw labor, or, in some studies, aggregated with physical capital (Kenen (1965)) into one capital variable to explain the Leontief paradox. Most researchers in recent years follow the first procedure of a separate independent human capital variable. There appears to be some consensus in this literature on the positive influence of human capital and the negative influence of unskilled labor on net exports. These findings are generally consistent with the body of literature on occupational skills, in which U.S. exports are skill intensive.

However, it should be noted that this approach has shortcomings. Lane (1985) has presented evidence that the capitalized value of human capital approach reflects elements of monopoly power. She shows that the human capital measure is erroneously high in highly concentrated and unionized industries. However, correction for these elements of market power does not greatly affect her regression estimates of the effect of human capital, or other influences, on trade.

More recently, Krueger and Summers (1988) have shown that there are substantial inter-industry wage differentials. These differences are far stronger than the market structure or union effects Lane considers. Such findings are sufficient to make capitalized wage measures of human capital quite questionable. At any rate, this book follows the occupational classification strand of the literature, which is less directly affected by inter-industry wage differentials.

Branson and Monoyios, who performed analysis of their data with both the discounted wage differential and the skill class methods of measuring human capital noted multicollinearity problems with the former method because by definition the human capital and labor variables are not constructed independently. They report that this problem, however, was not severe in their work. Harkness (1978) also reported "severe collinearity problems." Thus, another advantage of the methodology adopted in this book is that many factor inputs can be examined at once, free from the multicollinearity problems associated with the methodology previously used in the literature to study such issues.

Whether the method of assessing export performance is in terms of the skill content of exports or the capitalized value of human capital, most recent studies have shown that the United States has had a comparative advantage in the production of goods which intensively use skilled labor and a comparative disadvantage in the production of goods which intensively use unskilled labor. If this pattern still exists, huge trade deficits could possibly be less worrisome or the problems would be different than if the skill composition of exports has altered.

But in recent years, as the U.S. merchandise trade deficit has grown, there has been renewed concern that unfavorable trade performance has changed the types as well as the quantity of job skills exported and imported. On average, the United States trade deficit was $6 billion in 1975, $35 billion in 1976-1980, and an unprecedented $123 billion in 1984, and $148.5 billion in 1985. Prior to these record trade deficits the highest trade deficit had been $69 billion in 1983.

As the magnitude of the trade deficit has grown, a key question is whether the quality of jobs at which American workers are employed as well as the quantity of jobs has changed as a result of poorer net export performance. One concern is that international trade is altering the composition of the American labor force from highly paid jobs, most often in manufacturing, to lower paid, less skilled jobs, often in the service sector. A related concern is that most employment growth is in high-tech industries and in services, thereby creating a bipolarization in the wage and employment structures.

THE DISTRIBUTION OF
EARNINGS AND TRADE

Perhaps the most explicit statement of the idea that trade is now affecting the U.S. occupational structure adversely is in Thurow (1986), as follows:

> A lack of international competitiveness(manifested in a $150 billion annual trade deficit(is eliminating some of America's best-paying jobs. The industries that pay the highest wages and thus help narrow inequalities are suffering the most from our lack of competitiveness. . . .

When imports rise and exports fall as they have in the
last five years, a large hunk is taken out of the middle of
the earnings distribution. Between 1980 and the middle
of 1985, for example, the rise in imports drove the
wages of 300,000 workers below $12,500 a year.[2]

The concern expressed by Thurow is part of the larger issue of the
present and future skill content of the U.S. work force expressed earlier
by Bluestone and Harrison (1982). More recently (1987), they state that
there has been a proliferation of low-wage employment. (Low-wage is
defined as jobs paying $7400 or less in 1986 dollars, which is half the
median wage in 1973, corrected for inflation; high-wage jobs pay more
than $29,600, twice the 1973 median when corrected for inflation.)

Bluestone and Harrison calculate that between 1979 and 1985, 9.3
million net new jobs were created; of these, 44 percent paid poverty-
level wages, which was more than twice the low-wage portion of total
jobs created in the 1960's and 1970's, and about 10 percent of the net
new jobs were in the high-wage category, which was one-third the high-
wage proportion of all jobs created between 1963 and 1979. During the
same period, the share of new jobs paying mid-level wages fell by
almost 30 percent. Bluestone and Harrison attribute these developments
in part to foreign imports and in part to the shift of the labor force out
of higher wage manufacturing into lower wage service industries; of
course, these influences are related since manufacturing is typically
much more affected by trade than services are.

Kutscher and Personick (1986) document a relative shift towards
service industries in the past 25 years, which has intensified in recent
years, partly because of import penetration in manufacturing. In 1959,
the goods-producing sector accounted for 40 percent of all jobs, and the
service sector, 60 percent. By 1984, the goods-producing sector
accounted for 27 percent, and the service sector had increased to 72
percent of all jobs. The manufacturing share of employment fell from
25 to 18 percent over the same period, remaining level in absolute
terms at 19 to 20 million jobs. From 1979 to the 1983 trough,
employment declined by 3 million in the goods-producing sector, and
by 2.6 million in the manufacturing portion of the goods category.
Goods-producing employment rose by 1.4 million by 1984, but
manufacturing employment was still 1.6 million lower than in 1979.
Services increased each year from 1979 to 1984 by a total of 7 million
jobs.

Kutscher and Personick, using data for 1969 and 1984, single out
as in "deep trouble" a group of industries which experienced heavy
employment losses and a 20 percent decline in output over the 15 year

period. These include steel, some mining, wooden containers, rubber products except tires, leather products, primary nonferrous metals and products, heating equipment and plumbing fixtures, railroad equipment, and watches and clocks. These industries accounted for 6.7 percent of total real production in 1969, and 3.7 percent in 1984.

In addition to these long-term declining industries, several other industries never recovered from the 1982 recession. Production in the following industries was still at least 10 percent below pre-recession levels in 1984: fabricated structural metal; cutlery and hand tools; engines and turbines; farm and garden machinery; construction, mining, and oil field machinery; electrical transmission equipment; and electrical industrial apparatus.

Thus Kutscher and Personick assert that imports of manufactured goods have hastened the decline of the relative importance of manufacturing employment and establish some industries in which employment declines were particularly severe. Schoepfle (1982) also analyzes import penetration and identifies "import-sensitive" industries, which constitute one-quarter of all manufacturing industries in which workers might be adversely affected by foreign trade. Neither Kutscher and Personick nor Schoepfle address the question of whether this import-induced decline in the relative importance of manufacturing jobs means the United States is losing better jobs to trade.

If the United States were losing good jobs, the proportion of employment in the top and middle third of the job categories in terms of earnings would decline, and the proportion in the bottom third would increase. For bipolarization to occur, the proportion in the middle third would decline, and the bottom and top thirds would show an increase. Various researchers who have examined whether the proportion of wage earners in these groups has changed have come to different conclusions.

Rosenthal (1985) looked at median weekly earnings between 1973 and 1982 by occupation and found that (1) the proportion of high-paying jobs increased; (2) there was a slight shift away from middle-paying jobs; and (3) the proportion of lower paying jobs declined. In contrast, Lawrence (1985) analyzed earnings distributions between 1969 and 1983 and found the proportion of lower paying jobs increased.

Rosenthal arrayed 416 detailed occupations in 1982 by usual weekly earnings and arranged them into thirds, with each third containing the same number of occupations, summed the number of workers in the occupations in each third, and calculated a percent distribution of employment. He then arrayed employment in 1973 for each occupation in the same order as in 1982, and calculated the 1973 percent distribution for each third. Lawrence approached the question by distributing workers into earnings classes that are a fixed percentage of the median full-time worker weekly earnings. This method differs from the occupational method in that that method assumes that the earnings levels, rather than the "class" of occupations which divide workers into classes, is fixed.

McMahon and Tschetter (1986) replicated and updated both the Rosenthal and Lawrence studies with data for 1973 to 1985 and found, consistent with Rosenthal, a declining proportion of employment in lower paying jobs with Rosenthal's occupational approach and, consistent with Lawrence, an increasing proportion of lower paying jobs with Lawrence's earnings approach. (Both methods yielded a decline in the proportion of the middle third. The occupational approach showed an increase in high-paying jobs; the earnings approach a decrease over the study period.)

McMahon and Tschetter conclude that at the root of the disparity was a downward shift in the earnings distribution within the occupational groupings, so that, for example, the proportion of workers classified in the top occupational category who fell in the top earnings category declined from 1973 to 1982, while the proportion of workers in the middle and bottom wage categories formerly in the top occupational group increased. A similar downward displacement held for each of the three occupational groupings. These authors were not able to identify the cause of these changes in the earnings distribution.

One way to determine whether, in fact, the earnings distribution has shifted downward as claimed would be to compare the average earnings in each occupation over the years studied in this book, for example, 1977 to 1985. To relate such shifts to this book, if such data were available, it would then be possible to ascertain how much of any earnings decline was attributable to international trade by correlating the percent decline in average earnings in each occupation with the changes in the corresponding R value for the occupation generated as outlined above. Unfortunately, measures of average income in each of the detailed occupation groups are not available over the study period to determine whether trade effects were important in reducing the average income within particular occupational categories. In the absence of data on income changes within occupations, we adopt the occupation as the unit of observation in this book, which is consistent with Rosenthal's framework.

What the regression methodology outlined in Section 3 will determine is how the net trade flows in factor services are associated with the central characteristics of occupations, earnings and education. This is the first study examining sufficient skills to econometrically test hypotheses concerning the relationship between trade and "good" jobs, as defined by standard criteria.

Finally, as Grinols and Matusz (1988) point out, economic theory has not yet paid much attention to the potential role of foreign trade in eliminating the best domestic jobs. On the basis of the common evidence that United States foreign trade creates jobs for highly skilled occupational groups such as professional managerial workers and destroys jobs for operatives, it is plausible to interpret the evidence as indicating that foreign trade on balance creates good jobs for United States workers. Grinols and Matusz provide a theoretical argument that trade liberalization "can cause workers to move out of high-paying jobs and into low-paying jobs, as long as their relative ability in the high-paying job is low enough." Since this article has demonstrated that trade can theoretically either create or destroy good jobs for United States workers, the issue is an empirical matter and must be addressed by empirical methods.

The Grinols-Matusz analysis also emphasizes the role of education, since this is presumably a key variable in determining an individual's flexibility, and, therefore, how good the alternative job to which he might be shifted is. For individuals with high human capital, formal education is presumably a greater share of their overall human capital than their specific job training. Therefore, they should be less hurt by trade since their next best occupation will be comparatively good. However, for less educated groups, their specific job training will be a greater part of their overall human capital, and this is more likely to be extinguished by trade disruption. Therefore, less educated workers can be expected to be more likely to be hurt by trade.

In summary, this book is very much compatible with the Grinols-Matusz line of work in that they suggest that the displacement of good jobs is essentially an empirical matter, and that the effects may be quite different for different educational groups. This book conducts empirical tests such as those Grinols-Matusz suggest is necessary, and also distinguishes between different educational groups which Grinols-Matusz suggest is a key component of worker flexibility and therefore also of the empirical results which emerge.

THE INTERPRETATION OF WAGE DIFFERENTIALS

Occupations can differ in wages for many different reasons. For example, some reasons which might cause wages to differ between occupations are (1) distasteful work, (2) unmeasured labor skills, (3) location in high cost-of-living areas, (4) short or fluctuating hours, (5) unions, (6) firm concentration, (7) factory size, (8) occupational misclassification.

The first four items on this list would not represent genuine welfare differences between jobs, and therefore could represent cases in which there are compensation differences, but these do not reflect on how good a specific occupation is. For example, a construction worker may receive high hourly pay, but this may reflect the danger of injury on the job (item (1) on the above list) or the intermittent nature of employment in this industry (item 4). (However, the latter factor is somewhat mitigated since we consider only full-time workers; nevertheless the general level of pay, including that of the relatively few full-time workers may be raised by the possibility of frequent job interruption.)

It is difficult to reach a quantitative overall understanding of how important each of the factors listed above is in determining occupational differentials. There is a fairly considerable literature examining the effect of many of these influences, such as the presence of unions or the susceptibility to injury of individual jobs. Nevertheless, an overall evaluation would require data on each of the items, in order to sort out the relationships between them and the separate influence of each. Such comprehensive data do not exist, although the influence of some of the requisite variables can be taken into account in some of the commonly used micro data sets, such as the *Current Population Survey.*

In many cases, individual occupations are concentrated in one or a few industries, and therefore to a considerable extent occupational differentials are likely to reflect inter-industry wage differentials. Recently there has been a lot of work on inter-industry wage differentials. As Krueger and Summers (1988) demonstrate, inter-industry wage differentials are very large and persist over time. Comparable workers in the investment securities business get paid very much more than their counterparts in retail trade. Moreover, workers in all occupations within an industry receive similar premiums over similar workers in other industries; high pay for blue-collar workers in an industry is correlated with pay for professional and clerical workers in that industry. These difference are even similar in different countries.

The most recent work in the literature has focused on three main theories to explain these persistent wage differentials: (1) compensating differentials, (2) unmeasured differences in ability, and (3) efficiency wage theories.

The compensating differential argument in this context is that agreeable and disagreeable job attributes vary systematically with one's industry of employment and therefore necessitate wage differentials to compensate for non-wage aspects of the industry. Many recent studies reject this line of thought. This literature commonly refers to the Krueger and Summers (1988) finding that fringe benefits accentuate rather than reduce wage differentials across industries. Krueger and Summers also analyze wage differentials in terms of ten job attributes, including weekly hours, presence and severity of hazards, second and third shift dummies, commuting time, overtime choice variables, and physical amenities variables. These working condition variables do not substantially alter the pattern of industry wages.

Moreover, as Dickens and Katz (1987) point out, if wage premiums reflect equalizing differences they do not reflect rents that make jobs especially valuable to workers. Therefore, industry wage premiums would not be expected to be systematically related to quit rates. Yet they cite industry and individual level studies which indicate that wage premiums are strongly associated with lower quit rates (Ulman (1965), Pencavel (1970), Freeman (1980), Dickens and Katz (1987), Katz and Summers (1987)).

The second major proposed explanation is ability differences. Krueger and Summers (1988) dismiss unmeasured ability differences. After controlling for sex and occupation, controlling for other skill variables such as education or experience has only a very small impact on wage dispersion. Moreover, they present longitudinal evidence that when individuals move between industries, either because of displacement or due to normal labor market processes, their wages change by amounts similar to the industry differentials estimated in cross-section regressions. They conclude: "Unless one believes that variation in unmeasured labor quality is vastly more important than variation in age, tenure, and schooling, [measured labor quality], [our] evidence makes it difficult to attribute inter-industry wage differences to differences in labor quality."[3] Footnote 8 to this text continues, "Evidence suggests that unmeasured ability and upbringing have surprisingly little power in explaining wages. For instance, results presented in Taubman (1977) suggested that the expected difference in earnings between identical twins is about two-thirds as great as between randomly chosen members of the population. Jencks (1972) reports similar results for a host of other variables."

The central characteristic of efficiency wage theories, the third contending explanation, is that some firms find it profitable to pay wages higher than the going rate of compensation. There are at least four conceptually distinct efficiency wage theories. The first and most well-known is the shirking model. Employers have imperfect information regarding the behavior of workers on the job, and supervision is costly. By increasing wages above opportunity costs, workers value their jobs and the threat of losing them for detected loafing is an incentive not to shirk. A second model postulates that efficiency wages are paid to minimize turnover costs. A third possibility is that higher wages attract higher quality job applicants. A fourth model (Akerlof 1984) is that workers are more loyal and hence more productive to the extent that the firm shares its profits with them.

Krueger and Summers (1988) find that reductions in turnover alone are not sufficient to justify wage premiums of the magnitude actually observed. Second, the fact that industry wage differences cut across occupational lines casts doubt on the shirking model since monitoring costs are likely to vary across occupations. Because it is unlikely that workers in different occupations within an industry have similar quantities of unmeasured ability they also rule out the unmeasured labor quality explanation. Krueger and Summers favor the productivity enhancement explanation. This class of efficiency wage theory is consistent with the existence of the industry wage differentials, the correlation of these differences between occupations, the correlation of the industry differences with profits and with concentration ratios, and the stability of these wage premiums over time.

The study by Bartel and Lichtenberg (1988) supports this line of thought. However, it also illustrates the difficulty of disentangling firm motivations. Bartel and Lichtenberg's work could be said to blend two of the efficiency wage arguments(use of higher wages both to attract the best workers and to elicit their best performance, but it also has elements of the unmeasured ability argument. They argue that higher wages are necessary to elicit increases in both ability and effort. They find that industries with a high rate of technical change, as measured by (1) age of equipment, (2) R&D to sales ratios, and (3) share of computer purchases to value of output, pay higher wages to workers of a given age and education. This is necessary because introduction of new technology creates a demand for learning and that learning is a function of employee ability and effort. Firms undergoing technical change will want to (1) employ the most talented people within education groups, and (2) elicit high levels of effort from workers.

Their study receives support from another quarter. The importance of wage policies as enhancing productivity was apparent in a discussion I had with my brother, who is a manager for a large chemical company. He stated that his company is one firm which stresses quality throughout all facets of its operation. The firm consistently attempts to get all workers to contribute their best effort. It attempts to hire the best workers and has a philosophy of paying them well. The emphasis at his establishment is on team effort in which all workers consistently try to cut costs. The idea is that when all members of the team are well paid, satisfied, and committed to the corporation, they will be able jointly through a team effort to greatly reduce costs or otherwise contribute to productivity growth Therefore, a committed effort by all members will greatly increase productivity growth.

The President of North American Honda, Tetsuo Chino, also emphasized the importance of positive attitudes toward workers as a major factor in a company's success. In the February 14, 1989 *New York Times*, he says:

> The American auto industry is getting stronger and stronger, particularly in the case of the Ford Motor Company. When I drove the Lincoln Continental I was surprised at the quality, the fit and finish, and the performance. This does not require Honda to change its strategy, but it means we must work harder. American people don't trust American labor. You have to trust American labor. I think Ford understands this.

Similarly, another example is J.P. Morgan's policy of hiring "the cream" and paying them highly in order to create a climate of excellence which fosters productivity.

The argument that inter-industry wage differentials are essentially directed at avoiding blue-collar shirking is not intuitively appealing for many portions of the economy. It makes little sense to argue that a firm like Merck, for example, pays its blue-collar workers highly merely to avoid shirking when its success is driven by outstanding white-collar performance. Firms of the type mentioned here have an organizational attitude which creates an esprit de corps, a climate of organizational quality which motivates everyone to do high quality work (Clague, 1977). Intrinsic to that aim is high pay and high self esteem which frees individuals to do their best. This unifying argument is much more plausible than the bifurcated conclusion Dickens and Katz come to that posits "shirking avoidance" as the motivation for the blue-collar segment of an industry's work force and "sociological reasons," such as fostering loyalty as the reason professionals and managers in the same establishments are also highly paid. Dickens and Katz themselves find it necessary to apologize for the clumsiness of these explanations.

Finally, it seems to me that if an employer took such a dim view of his employees as Lazear seems to believe he does, so that he pays them more highly merely to avoid their shirking, this negativism would certainly be transmitted to the workers and would hardly be a climate conducive to high productivity or even good work.

On the basis of this argument, the main factors in higher wages are organizational quality and technology. The more important element is organizational quality. Good organizations go out of their way to hire plant shows, it is organizational quality which is important. The General Motors Fremont plant had low productivity and high absenteeism and was in danger of being closed. With the same workers, the Toyota-run NUMMI plant is productive, absenteeism rates are low, and the plant will remain in production.

However, organizational quality alone is not enough. McDonald's is a very high quality organization with good industrial relations; nevertheless, the technology and associated skills in the fast-food industry are not sufficient to pay large numbers of workers high wages, although many franchises are very profitable. It is the combination of organizational quality and technology which appears necessary to pay high wages or create a good job. The nation would be much better off if more such good jobs could be created.

It is interesting that Katz and Summers (1988) find that industries with good jobs are successful in international trade in the sense that they export a lot, and industries with poor jobs typically import a lot. This is direct evidence that trade, on balance, creates good jobs, as also found in this book. Although closely related, the occupation and industry frameworks approach the issue from somewhat different viewpoints, so the evidence presented in this book is complementary to the Katz and Summers results. In addition, this book considers a broader range of evidence because it examines alternative years and alternative groups of workers, and examines evidence for the total economy within the factor requirements methodology characteristic of trade theory.

NOTES

1. Leamer and Bowen (1981) show that the regression approach does not necessarily indicate factor abundance. Define

T = an nx1 vector of the net exports of country i in each of n industries.

A = an mxn matrix in which a_{kj}, an element of the matrix, shows the total factor demands (direct plus indirect) of factor k required to deliver one unit of final demand for commodity j.

In the usual regressions,

$$T_i = A'Bi + u_i \quad (a)$$

in which the dependent variable is net trade in industry i and A' again reflects the total factor inputs required to produce one unit of final demand for each commodity.

Note that in any regression,

$$Y = a + bx \quad (b)$$

Expressed in matrix form, the regression coefficients b are

$$b = (X'X)^{-1}X'Y \quad (c)$$

with Y = T and X = A' in (a), (c) becomes

$$b = (AA')^{-1}AT$$

so that the coefficients b reflect the net export of factor services (AT) only if premultiplication by $(AA')^{-1}$ does not affect the signs indicated by AT. As Leamer and Bowen demonstrate with a counterexample, these conditions cannot be assured.

2. Lester Thurow, "The Hidden Sting of the Trade Deficit," *The New York Times,* January 19, 1986, p. D-3.

3. Alan B. Krueger and Lawrence H. Summers, "Efficiency Wages and the Inter-industry Wage Structure," *Econometrica,* (March 1988), p. 269.

II

Development of the Data Base

INTRODUCTION

This chapter describes the development of the data base constructed in order to conduct the tests described in Chapter I. The discussion includes information on the major data sources and on the types of transformations and data operations conducted to ensure that data gathered from the different sources are compatible.

The discussion in this chapter deals with five central topics. The first section describes the essential information on employment in each occupational category by industry. The second section discusses the total requirements of the input-output matrix, through which the information on occupational skills by industry is converted into measures of the total requirements of each skill required to supply one dollar to final demand from each industry. The third section considers the development of data on net exports for each industry in each year. The fourth section develops consistent and parallel data on deliveries to final demand from each industry in each year, which are used in calculating the total skill content contained in each year's pattern of national consumption. Finally, the fifth area is data on the income of full-time workers in each occupational category, which are used to categorize "good" jobs and determine whether trade has had a particularly strong impact on these occupations. Sections 2 through 8 of this Chapter discuss each of these topics.

INFORMATION ON OCCUPATIONAL
SKILLS BY INDUSTRY

The Office of Economic Growth of the Bureau of Labor Statistics provided the central information on employment in each occupation in each industry. The source is the occupation-by-industry matrix. This is by far the most detailed consistent data base available on this topic, and is the basis for the official employment projections prepared by the Bureau of Labor Statistics.

The BLS matrix is based on information from two sources. The first is the decennial *Census of Population* and the associated *Current Population Survey* information which is prepared from a continuous sequence of sample surveys, and is the source of much of the information used in national employment and labor force reports. The second source of information is surveys of occupational employment conducted by the Bureau of Labor Statistics. These are conducted every three or four years, on a rotating basis, and cover manufacturing, services, and other industries in turn. The Bureau staff blends the detailed information from these sources together, and prepares the BLS occupation by industry matrix. Since these data are based on the fullest most detailed individual plant level information ever available on this topic, they clearly represent the best, most reliable information ever available on this important topic. These detailed data do not appear to have been ever used in the academic economics literature.

The central data used in this book are the matrix data for 1984. They include wage and salary employment, which accounts for the great majority of the national labor force. Self-employed workers are not included.

THE SELF-EMPLOYED

The Census defines self-employed workers as those who work for profit or fees in their own unincorporated business, profession, or trade, or who operate a farm. This definition excludes (1) owners of incorporated businesses, (2) persons self-employed at second jobs who are classified in terms of their primary employment, and (3) unpaid family workers.

Self-employed workers numbered 8.2 million in 1979. They tend to be older, male, white and employed in white-collar or trade occupations (Fain, 1980). They tend to be older than wage and salary workers possibly because it takes time to acquire capital and managerial skills to start a business. The self-employed were more likely to be men than workers in general; 75 percent of the self-employed were men; 60 percent of wage and salary workers were men. Minorities are less likely to be self-employed: the proportion of black business owners has remained for years at 5.5 percent, and the blacks who are self-employed are more likely to be in service and blue-collar occupations, while white self-employed workers are more likely to be in white-collar occupations.

The proportion of workers self-employed in nonagricultural industries is about 7.1 percent. Service-producing industries account for most of these workers: 77.7 percent of all the self-employed are in service industries and 22.3 percent in goods-producing industries, as compared to wage and salary employment, in which 68 percent are in service industries, and 32 percent in goods-producing industries. Within services, 27.3 percent of self-employed workers versus 20.4 percent of wage and salary workers are in trade, especially retail (23.2 percent for self-employed and 20.4 percent of wage and salary employees). Another overrepresented sector was miscellaneous business services (39.8 percent of the self-employed compared to 28.5 percent of wage and salary workers). Within the goods-producing sector, the self-employed are concentrated in construction: 17 percent versus 5.9 percent for wage and salary employment.

In terms of occupation, the self-employed are most heavily concentrated in managerial, professional and craft occupations. For a small number of occupations, self employment accounted for more than half of all workers, including chiropractors, dentists, optometrists, podiatrists, authors, auctioneers, hucksters and peddlers, paper hangers, piano and organ tuners, shoe repairers, fishers, farmers, midwives, barbers, boarding and lodging housekeepers, and bootblacks. Seventeen percent of the self-employed are farmers, compared to 1.2 percent of wage and salary workers. This omission might by itself understate the magnitude of net exports, at least for farming occupations.

In prior years, self-employed workers were also distinguished by longer hours than their wage and salary counterparts, but the data reveal that by 1979, they worked an average of 41.9 hours, slightly more than the 38.4 hours logged by wage and salary employees. Mean earnings were higher for the self-employed, but are substantially skewed at the upper end of the earnings distribution. A number of self-employed persons earn very high salaries while the majority earn less than the average for wage and salary employees. It is suspected that there is also some underreporting of income among those who work for themselves. Finally, the self-employed do not experience as severe cyclical swings in employment as do employees, but tend to absorb losses in downturns rather than abandoning their businesses.

COMPRESSION OF THE DATA BASE

The available matrix information on employed workers refers to 560 occupations in 325 industries. Two types of transformations have to be conducted to make these data useful for this book. First, the 325 industries refer to Standard Industrial Classification (SIC) industries. Most of the industries considered are at the three-digit level of the SIC.

These industries have to be converted to an input-output (IO) classification, so that total occupational requirements can appropriately be calculated through the input-output methodology.

The 325 industries contained in the matrix data base are compressed to the 156 sectors described in Section 5 of the data discussion. In most instances, the SIC industries in the matrix data base can easily be converted to their input-output equivalent, as listed in the equivalence table given in the beginning pages of any published input-output table.

However, in some cases, a single BLS SIC industry is split up into two or several of the 156 relevant input-output sectors. For example, a typical SIC industry in the matrix refers to a three-digit industry. In some cases, a given four-digit industry within a given three-digit observation may be assigned to one IO sector, another four-digit sector to another IO sector, and still another four-digit industry to a third IO sector. In these circumstances, the employment in the three-digit industry is divided in proportion to the wage and salary employment in each of the four-digit subcategories and assigned to the corresponding IO sector. For example, 20 percent may be assigned to the first IO sector, 50 percent to a second, and 30 percent to a third. The 1984 wage and salary employment for these subindustries is obtained from the Economic Growth Project database computer listings or from the 1984 issue of the Bureau of Labor Statistics publication *Employment and Earnings.*

Since the BLS matrix is typically available at the three-digit industry level, no information usually exists on the occupational composition of skills at the detailed four-digit industry level. Therefore, the distribution of occupational skills is assumed to be the same within each four-digit industry as within a given three-digit category. This same bundle or distribution of occupational skills is assigned to each of the three recipient input-output industries. Only the employment total assigned to each four-digit industry varies among the different component SIC industries.

In addition to the compression from the 325 SIC industries to the 156 IO sectors, the data on 560 occupations was reduced to the 134 major occupational categories used in the 1980 *Census of Population*, as discussed in Section 8 of this chapter. (As discussed later, the final analysis involved 118 occupations.) This makes it possible to use the *Census of Population* information on income in each occupation and income in each educational category for each occupation category to define "good" jobs, and to associate these data with the results from the trade analysis. The 134 occupational category distribution was used because the *Census of Population* information is available at this level of detail. In some instances, it would have been possible to include a larger number of distinct occupational categories, but this would have involved using a mixture of *Census of Population* minor group and individual occupational data, rather than an established Census level of occupational detail. In addition, the limitation to 134 distinct occupational categories made it feasible to conduct the tests reported here with the available computer resources.

In actuality, employment in 12 of the 134 major occupational groups was zero, either because the group was self-employed, whereas this book includes only wage and salary workers, or because a given occupation did not fit into any of the 560 occupational titles. Therefore, the analysis conducted refers to 122 or, for other reasons explained later, 118 of the 134 major occupational categories.

INFORMATION ON THE TOTAL
REQUIREMENTS INPUT-OUTPUT TABLE

The calculations required for this book must be based on the total requirements version of the input-output table, which includes both the direct and indirect factor requirements necessary to deliver a unit of final demand.

All calculations are based on the 156 order input-output table used by the Office of Economic Growth of the Bureau of Labor Statistics. The total requirements version of the Office of Economic Growth tables is used.

The table used is fundamentally based on the 1977 national input-output table produced by the Bureau of Economic Analysis. Since the input-output structure used is for 1977, the technology used for this book actually refers to several years earlier than the 1982 to 1985 period for which the central information for the rest of this book is based. However, it is common to analyze an input-output table referring to a year some years in the past in the trade and input-output literature. For example, Sveikauskas (1983) and Bowen, Leamer, and Sveikauskas (1987) both used a 1967 input-output table to study the issues they considered, although these studies both appeared in the 1980's. The reason, of course, is the long delay which occurs before U.S. input-output tables become available. The studies cited use the 1967 technology matrix with consistent 1967 trade information. The present study similarly analyzes 1977 trade with 1977 technology. However, 1982 and 1985 trade are also analyzed with 1977 technology because no comparable information is available on technology in later years. In combining the occupational skill information from Section 2 with the total requirements input-output information from Section 5, particular care is taken to ensure consistency with the fact that the input-output table refers to 1977. The skills required per dollar of output in each industry are obtained by dividing 1984 employment in each occupation in each industry by 1984 output in that same industry, but the 1984 output in that industry is measured in constant 1977 dollars. Therefore, the skills required per dollar of output in each industry are directly compatible with the input-output table which is in 1977 dollars. Similarly, the data on net exports and total national consumption discussed in Sections 6 and 7 are both also consistently measured in 1977 dollars.

The calculations required to determine the total amount of a given skill needed to produce a dollar of output from a given industry can be summarized formally as follows:

$$Ai = sum\ tij\ (Si/Oi)$$

The total output requirement from industry i needed to deliver a single unit of output to industry j, tij, is multiplied by the employment in a particular skill in that industry divided by output and summed over each of the i industries, i=1 to 156. As mentioned above, skills are measured in 1984 employment and 1984 output in each industry in 1977 dollars. Therefore, the contribution from each industry i is tij(Si/Oi) in which S_i is employment of that skill in industry i and O_i is output in industry i. The total requirements are calculated by adding the requirements over each of the 156 industries.

Similar calculations are made to determine the total requirements of that skill for each of the j or 156 commodities. Parallel calculations are conducted for each of the other 117 skill categories, since 118 skills in all are examined.

The total occupational requirements are calculated as numbers of individual workers in each skill required per million dollars of output (in 1977 dollars). The net export and consumption data described below are also measured in millions of 1977 dollars. Consequently, when the total requirements data (in workers per million) are later multiplied by net exports or consumption (in millions) the result is workers required for each bundle in numbers of individual workers.

DATA ON NET EXPORTS

Information on net exports in each of the 156 industries was fundamentally also obtained from the Office of Economic Growth of the Bureau of Labor Statistics. The BLS prepared information on net exports in 1977, 1982, and 1985 in constant 1982 dollars in each of

226 different industries. The 226-order data reflect the fact that the Economic Growth Project changed its sectoring plan to generate greater industry detail after this book was well under way. (Most of the new industry detail is in construction and services.)

In most cases, the 226 sectors in the new BLS classification scheme can unambiguously be assigned to a single one of the 156 industries considered here. However, 17 of the 226 sectors had to be split up into two industries, and 4 of the 226 sectors had to be divided up into three of the 156 industries.

In these cases, we allocated the net export data for these sectors to specific industries, based on information from the U. S. Department of Commerce International Trade Administration data base, which is also the primary source for most of the data contained in the Economic Growth Project's trade databank. In addition, we used some comparable data from an International Trade Commission report (Rousslang and Parks (1986)) to provide supplementary information for several industries outside manufacturing.

After all these calculations were conducted, the result was a measure of net exports for each of the 156 industries in 1977, 1982 and 1985 in 1982 dollars. These data were converted to 1977 dollars, using industry output deflators, to ensure consistency with the 1977 input-output definition of output.

DELIVERIES TO NATIONAL CONSUMPTION

As remarked in Chapter I, national consumption is measured by all deliveries to final demand except net exports. Data on deliveries to final demand are also available for 226 sectors from the BLS Economic Growth Project. Data are also for 1977, 1982 and 1985 in 1982 dollars.

As was the case in Section 6, 205 of the 226 Economic Growth sectors fit in a specific one of our 156 industries. In the remaining industries, final demand for 1977 is split among industries according to the national consumption of goods from each four-digit industry, as based upon information contained in the 496 order version of the 1977 input-output tables. The deliveries to final demand contained in this four-digit 1977 input-output table are also the basis for the Economic Growth Project data work and for the Economic Growth projections on final demand.

For 1982 and 1985 each four-digit industry's deliveries to consumption (final demand except for net exports) are allowed to increase with the growth of each industry's shipments. The Economic Growth Project data on deliveries to national consumption in 1982 and 1985 are allocated among industries on the basis of the 1977 consumption figures, adjusted for differential industry output growth between 1977 and 1982 or 1985. The estimates of deliveries to national consumption in each of the 156 industries are then also converted to 1977 constant dollars using the output price deflator for each industry also used for the net export data.

In many of the cases, the allocations between industries involve the assignment of most of a sector to one industry and a small amount to a different industry. In these cases, even considerable changes in the allocation procedure, say from a 90 and 10 split to an 85 and 15 split, would probably not have a substantial impact on the actual results. In other cases, potential differences in the allocation procedure could have a more important impact. However, even allowing for these cases, the allocation procedure described here is used in only a few cases so that alternative allocation procedures are unlikely to have a strong impact on results.

DATA ON INCOMES AND EDUCATION IN EACH OCCUPATION

The 134 occupations which are considered are those listed as Intermediate Occupational Classification (134) Items in Appendix A of the 1980 *Census of Population* publication *Occupation by Industry* (Subject Reports, Volume 2, Publication 7c). The same appendix also indicates the component individual occupations included within each of these intermediate classifications.

Subject Report 8B of the 1980 *Census of Population, Earnings by Occupation and Education,* Table 1 provides earnings of full-time and part-time workers in many different occupations in 1979. Further detail is available for full-time workers, including a cross-classification by sex and six educational categories (0 to 8 years, 1 to 3 years of high school, 4 years of high school, 1 to 3 years of college, 4 years of college, and 5 or more years of college). In addition, mean hourly earnings of full-time workers in each of these sex and education categories are also provided, as well as estimates of mean annual earnings for each of the categories.

Since the detailed occupations listed in Appendix A of the *Occupation by Industry* volume are essentially those for which earnings are given in the *Earnings by Occupation and Income* volume, these data can be combined and used to generate a variety of measures of what a "good job" is. One qualification, however, is that the earnings data refer to all employed workers, including the self-employed and other members of the Recent Experienced Civilian Labor Force, rather than just the wage and salary workers included in the BLS occupation by industry matrix.

The *Earnings by Occupation and Education* volume of the *Census of Population* contains information on the employment, average hourly wage, and annual income for workers in a large number of occupations. For 94 of the 134 occupational categories, this information is directly published in that volume. In the remaining 40 occupational groups, equivalent information was developed by aggregating similar information from the listings of individual occupations as described below.

For each occupation, information is obtained for full-time workers in six educational categories (elementary school, 1 to 3 years of high school, high school graduates, 1 to 3 years of college, college graduates, and additional years of college education). Separate information is also published for men and women. This information includes the number of males, male average hourly earnings, and male average annual income, the number of females, female average hourly earnings, and female average annual income. The average annual income data is necessary, since full-time workers of different educational groups and sexes work a different number of annual hours, and thus average hourly earnings cannot be calculated merely by weighting average hourly earnings by the number of workers.

In the first set of calculations conducted for each occupation, the number of hours worked by men and women in each educational category is determined by dividing average annual income by average hourly earnings. The data for employment hours and earnings for men and women is then combined to calculate the actual average hourly wage for all full-time workers within each educational category for each occupation.

Similar calculations are conducted to determine the average hourly wage for all workers in an occupation and the specific average hourly wage within each of the six educational categories.

These data are then used to calculate eight measures of the average hourly wage within each occupational category. The first concept is simply the average hourly wage for all full-time workers in the occupation divided by the corresponding average hourly wage of all full-time workers in the total experienced civilian labor force ($7.5355). The third measure is the average hourly wage of all full-time workers in the occupation with an elementary school education, divided by the corresponding wage for all full-time workers in this category in the total economy ($5.6149). Items four, five, six, seven, and eight calculate corresponding average wages for some high school, high school graduates, some college, college graduates, and postgraduate education, in each case again dividing by the corresponding national figures ($6.1286, 6.6449, 7.5350, 10.0062, 11.9540); these relative wage ratios are calculated for each occupation. Finally, measure two provides a weighted summary of items three through eight, in which the weights are the percent of employees in the work force in each education category. This concept provides a measure of how good the income in each job is, given the overall educational attainment in each occupation, which is one plausible definition of a good job. In addition, items three through eight provide information on how good a job is for certain specific education categories, which is a useful calculation since job displacement is often thought to be a particular problem for workers with only an elementary or high school education.

LEVEL OF OCCUPATIONAL DETAIL

Another matter which must be addressed before the data analysis can proceed is that at the level of detail considered, the 1980 *Census of Population* information on *Earnings by Occupation* distinguishes between 134 occupational groups within the total labor force. These 134 categories are described on pages A-8 to A-12 of volume 7C of the Subject Reports of the 1980 *Census of Population*. The level of occupational detail used in this book is reproduced in Table 2.2.

However, within the data on employment by occupation and industry used here, it is only possible to distinguish data on 118 separate occupational categories. In most instances, this compression of the available sample from 134 to 118 occurs because the employment data are not able to differentiate between different categories of managers and supervisors. For example, financial managers (item 2 of the 134 category list), marketing managers (item 3), and medical managers (item 5) are all mixed together with managers, not elsewhere classified (item 7) in the employment data and therefore in the net export and consumption series; similarly, managers, not elsewhere classified, self-employed (item 8) is simply omitted because the present sample is restricted to employed workers. Salaried sales supervisors (item 45), administrative support supervisors (item 52), mechanical and repair supervisors (item 80), production supervisors (item 93), material moving supervisors (item 124), and cleaning and labor supervisors (item 128) all inescapably have to be mixed in with construction supervisors (item 86); in addition, self-employed supervisors (item 46) are omitted. Altogether, this compression of the managers and supervisors data accounts for eleven of the sixteen categories in which no data are included in the present study.

Table 2.1. Definitions of Relative Wages for Each Occupational Group

Measure	Definition
Average Earnings	Average hourly wage for all full-time workers in the occupation, divided by the average hourly wage of all full-time workers in the labor force
Weighted Average Earnings	Weighted summary of items of the next six measures; the weights are the percent of employees in the education group
Earnings of Elementary Graduates	Earnings of elementary graduates in the occupation compared to the earnings of all workers with an elementary education
Earnings of High School Dropouts	Earnings of high school dropouts in the occupation compared to the earnings of all workers who dropped out of high school
Earnings of High School Graduates	Earnings of high school graduates in the occupation compared to the earnings of all workers who are high school graduates
Earnings of College Dropouts	Earnings of college dropouts in the occupation compared to the earnings of all workers who are college dropouts
Earnings of College Graduates	Earnings of college graduates in the occupation compared to the earnings of all workers who are college graduates
Earnings of Graduate School Attenders	Earnings of workers who attended graduate school in the occupation compared to the earnings of all workers with graduate school education

In the other five instances, two of the 134 categories are simply combined. These are systems analysts (item 21) and operations analysts (item 22); finance and services sales (item 47) and commodities sales (item 48); graders and sorters (item 118) and other production inspectors (item 119); truck drivers (item 120) and driver-sales workers (item 121); and construction laborers (item 130) and laborers except construction (item 134). In all these instances, the earnings data for individual occupational categories are aggregated in the same way that the corresponding employment data had to be aggregated, in order to maintain consistency between the relevant trade and consumption employment and the corresponding earnings information. Consequently, the tables in the next chapter are limited to the relevant 118 of the 134 occupational categories, consistently aggregated as described above.

Table 2.2 Census Occupational Classification, 134 Occupations

1. Officials and Administrators
2. Financial Managers
3. Managers, marketing, advertising, and public relations
4. Administrators, education and related fields
5. Managers, medicine and health
6. Other specified managers
7. Managers and administrators, nec, salaried
8. Managers and administrators, nec, self-employed
9. Accountants and auditors
10. Personnel, training, and labor relations specialists
11. Buyers and purchasing agents
12. Inspectors and compliance officers
13. Other management related occupations
14. Architects
15. Civil engineers
16. Electrical and electronic engineers
17. Industrial engineers
18. Mechanical engineers
19. Other engineers
20. Surveyors and mapping scientists
21. Computer systems analysts and scientists
22. Operations and systems researchers and analysts
23. Mathematical scientists
24. Chemists, except biochemists
25. Other natural scientists
26. Health diagnosing occupations
27. Registered nurses
28. Other health assessment and treating occupations
29. Teachers, except postsecondary
30. Social scientists and urban planners
31. Social and recreation workers
32. Lawyers and judges
33. Writers, artists, entertainers, and athletes
34. Other professional specialty occupations
35. Licensed practical nurses
36. Other health technologists and technicians
37. Electrical and electronic technicians
38. Industrial and mechanical engineering technicians
39. Drafting and surveying technicians
40. Other engineering and scientific technicians
41. Airplane pilots and navigators

Table 2.2 Census Occupational Classification (cont.)

42. Air traffic controllers
43. Computer programmers
44. Other technicians, except health, engineering, and science
45. Supervisors and proprietors, sales occupations, salaried
46. Supervisors and proprietors, sales occupations, self-employed
47. Sales representatives, finance and business services
48. Sales representatives, commodities except retail
49. Cashiers
50. Other sales occupations, retail and personal services
51. Sales related occupations
52. Supervisers, administrative support occupations
53. Computer equipment operators
54. Secretaries
55. Stenographers and typists
56. Receptionists
57. Other information clerks
58. File clerks
59. Other records processing, except financial
60. Bookkeepers, accounting and auditing clerks
61. Payroll and timekeeping clerks
62. Other financial records processing occupations
63. Telephone operators
64. Mail and message distributing occupations
65. Production coordinators and expeditors
66. Traffic, shipping, and receiving clerks
67. Stock and inventory clerks
68. Other material record, scheduling, and distributing clerks
69. Adjusters and investigators
70. Data-entry keyers
71. Other administrative support occupations
72. Private household occupations
73. Guards
74. Other protective service occupations
75. Food preparation and service occupations
76. Health service occupations
77. Cleaning and building service occupations, except household
78. Personal service occupations
79. Farming, forestry, and fishing occupations
80. Supervisers, mechanics, and repairers
81. Automobile mechanics
82. Industrial machinery repairers

Table 2.2 Census Occupational Classification (cont.)

83. Electronic repairers, communications and industry equipment
84. Heating, air conditioning, and refrigeration mechanics
85. Other mechanics and repairers
86. Supervisors, construction occupations
87. Carpenters
88. Electricians
89. Painters construction and maintainence
90. Plumbers, pipefitters, and steamfitters
91. Other construction trades
92. Extractive occupations
93. Supervisors, production occupations
94. Tool and die makers
95. Machinists
96. Sheet metal workers
97. Other precision metal workers
98. Precision textile, apparel, and furnishing machinery workers
99. Precision food production occupations
100. Precision inspectors, testers, and related workers
101. Plant and system operators
102. Other precision production occupations
103. Metalworking and plastic working machine operators
104. Fabricating machine operators, not elsewhere classified
105. Metal and plastic processing and woodworking machine operators
106. Printing machine operators
107. Textile machine operators
108. Textile sewing machine operators
109. Laundering and dry cleaning machine operators
110. Packaging and filling operators
111. Furnace, kiln, and oven machine operators, except food
112. Other specified machine operators
113. Miscellaneous and not specified machine operators
114. Welders and cutters
115. Solderers and brazers
116. Assemblers
117. Hand-working occupations
118. Graders and sorters, except agricultural
119. Other production inspectors, samplers, and weighers
120. Truck drivers
121. Driver-sales workers
122. Other motor vehicle operators
123. Rail and water transportation workers

Table 2.2 Census Occupational Classification (cont.)

124. Supervisors, material moving equipment operators
125. Crane, hoist, and winch operators
126. Excavating, grading, and dozer machine operators
127. Other material equipment moving operators
128. Supervisors: handlers, equipment cleaners, and laborers, nec
129. Helpers, craft and production
130. Construction laborers
131. Freight, stock, and material handlers
132. Garage and service station occupations, and equipment cleaners
133. Hand packers and packagers
134. Laborers, except construction

III

Data Analysis

INTRODUCTION

The first task was to calculate, for each of the 118 occupations, the jobs contained in net exports, the jobs required for domestic consumption (C), and the ratio of these jobs (NX/C), which is called R. (See Chapter 1.) The results of these calculations for one occupation, accountants and auditors, are displayed in Table 3.1a.

For example, in Table 3.1a, occupation 9 refers to accountants and auditors. The results show that, based on 1977 technology, the services produced by 3,412 accountants and auditors were exported in 1977, which increased to 13,204 in 1982. However, by 1985 the services of 10,117 accountants and auditors were imported. National consumption of accountants and auditors increased from 596,000 jobs in 1977 to 638,000 in 1982 and 744,000 in 1985. As a result, net exports as a percentage of consumption, or R, for accountants and auditors increased from .0057 in 1977 to .0207 in 1982, but declined to -.0136 in 1985. For job category 116, assemblers, net imports rose from 24,365 jobs in 1977 to 38,953 jobs in 1982 to 208,504 jobs in 1985. Consequently, R for assemblers declined from -.0247 in 1977 to -.0399 in 1982 to -.1545 in 1985, meaning greater import penetration and job loss. (See Table 3.1b.)

These data are given for all 118 occupations in Appendix 1. The R values for the 118 occupations are presented in Table 3.2.

OVERALL PATTERNS

This subsection develops an initial overview of the information in Table 3.2 on the ratio of jobs involved in net exports to jobs in consumption for each occupation for each year. The present discussion considers the broad pattern of results across the 118 individual occupations.

Table 3.1a Illustrative Table for Accountants and Auditors

Year	Jobs in Net Exports	Jobs in Consumption	R Value R=NX/C
1977	3,412	595,793	.0057
1982	13,204	638,283	.0207
1985	-10,117	744,430	-.0136

Table 3.1b Illustrative Table for Assemblers

Year	Job in Net Exports	Jobs in Consumption	R Value R=NX/C
1977	-24,365	988,123	-.0247
1982	-38,953	975,631	-.0399
1985	-208,504	-1,349,960	-.1545

Of the 118 occupations used in this study, R values were positive in each of the years 1977, 1982 and 1985 in 16 occupations. These are generally white-collar occupations, and appear to be jobs not usually considered directly involved in international trade. Sample occupations are physicians, lawyers, architects, and civil engineers. Among less skilled groups, sales workers in finance and business services, cashiers, other sales workers, information clerks, stock clerks, adjusters and investigators, and other administrative support workers all fall into this category. Farm workers and private household workers (some of whom are employed in business services, and therefore do not supply their services solely to consumption) also fall into this category. Even among occupations in this always-positive category, however, the trade contribution to jobs was far less in 1985 than in previous years. For example, the ratio of net exports to consumption was .0145 for civil engineers in 1977 and .0217 in 1982, but declined to only .0017 in 1985.

For twenty-one occupations R was negative for each of the three years. These occupations were mainly for blue-collar workers, particularly in the precision production and operatives categories. Typical occupational categories were metal and plastic processors, wood machine operators, textile machine operators, assemblers, and furnace, kiln, and oven operators; among more skilled blue-collar groups precision textile operators, plumbers, electricians, and plant and system operators were imported in each year. Some white-collar jobs also fall into the category in which R is negative in each year; education and related administrators, other physical scientists, and payroll and timekeepers all fall into this group.

The largest group of occupations, 69 of the 118 occupations considered, had positive net exports in 1977 and 1982, but shifted over to a surplus of imports in 1985. Of course, this reflects the trade deficit, which was mildly negative in 1977 and 1982 (with merchandise trade deficits of $39 billion in 1977 and $43 billion in 1982) but was very large in 1985 (with a merchandise trade deficit of $148 billion). For another 15 occupations, R values were positive in 1982, but negative in 1977 and 1985. Exports of the services of a few other occupations swung into deficit earlier, from 1977 to 1982.

Table 3.2 Ratio of Jobs in Net Exports/Jobs in Consumption,
          1977, 1982, 1985.

1977	1982	1985		Occupation number and title
Executive, administrative, and managerial occupations				
0.00000	0.00000	0.00000	1	Officials, administrators
-0.00013	-0.00006	-0.00048	4	Administrators, education
0.01034	0.01433	0.01350	6	Other specified managers
0.00371	0.01122	0.01420	7	Managers, nec., salaried
0.00573	0.02069	-0.01359	9	Accountants, auditors
0.00095	0.00785	-0.01378	10	Personnel specialists
0.02175	0.02696	-0.00881	11	Buyers, purchasing agents
0.00042	0.00113	-0.00099	12	Inspectors, compliance officers
0.02132	0.02456	-0.01825	13	Other managers
Professional specialty occupations				
0.05133	0.05978	0.02283	14	Architects
0.01454	0.02171	0.00173	15	Civil engineers
0.03487	0.04492	-0.02751	16	Electrical engineers
0.03077	0.03233	-0.05821	17	Industrial engineers
0.04783	0.04855	-0.03766	18	Mechanical engineers
-0.01457	0.01297	-0.04640	19	Other engineers
-0.00691	0.02154	-0.00511	20	Surveyors
0.00675	0.02102	-0.01596	21	Systems analysts
-0.00490	0.00567	-0.01406	23	Mathematicians
-0.00705	0.01548	-0.04277	24	Chemists
-0.07357	-0.02916	-0.04512	25	Other physical scientists
0.00242	0.00250	0.00071	26	Health diagnosing occupations
0.00079	0.00106	-0.00016	27	Registered nurses
0.00054	0.00073	-0.00016	28	Other health occupations
-0.00008	0.00006	-0.00085	29	Teachers
-0.00139	0.00289	-0.00254	30	Social scientists
0.00149	0.00212	-0.00007	31	Social workers
0.02643	0.03493	0.01156	32	Lawyers
0.01201	0.01715	-0.00974	33	Writers, artists
0.00062	0.00106	-0.00036	34	Other professionals

Table 3.2 (cont.)

Technicians and related support occupations

0.00167	0.00205	-0.00013	35	Licensed prac nurses
0.00035	0.00033	-0.00261	36	Other health technicians
0.03984	0.05239	-0.00962	37	Electronics technicians
0.03711	0.07348	-0.06585	38	Industrial technicians
0.02092	0.03311	-0.03812	39	Drafting technicians
-0.01573	0.00266	-0.06356	40	Other science engineering techs

Technicians and related support occupations

-0.00455	0.02268	-0.02581	41	Airplane pilots
0.00758	0.00839	-0.00440	42	Controllers
0.01314	0.02851	-0.01556	43	Computer programmers
0.00676	0.01353	-0.00276	44	Other technicians

Sales occupations

0.00732	0.01319	0.00528	47	Sales reps, finance & business
0.00519	0.00683	0.00179	49	Cashiers
0.00871	0.01054	0.00483	50	Other sales, retail/pers. services
0.03451	0.03991	0.00460	51	Sales occupations

Table 3.2 (cont.)

Administrative support occupations including clerical

0.00568	0.01824	-0.01224	53	Computer operators
0.00822	0.01856	-0.01003	54	Secretaries
0.00815	0.00120	-0.00324	55	Stenographers/typists
0.00101	0.00762	-0.00627	56	Receptionists
0.01679	0.03064	0.00086	57	Other information clerks
0.00099	0.00956	-0.00656	58	File clerks
0.01666	0.02130	-0.00564	59	Other records clerks
0.00845	0.01585	-0.01031	60	Accounting clerks
-0.01388	-0.00743	-0.04232	61	Payroll clerks
0.02263	0.02521	0.00000	62	Other financial clerks
0.01856	0.01127	-0.00043	63	Telephone operators
0.01078	0.01539	-0.00998	64	Postal clerks/carriers
0.01517	0.01608	-0.06815	65	Production coordinators
0.02254	0.02372	-0.03683	66	Shipping clerks
0.02546	0.02847	0.00150	67	Stock/inventory clerks
0.00092	0.00451	-0.01904	68	Recording clerks
0.00830	0.01025	0.00406	69	Investigators
0.00186	0.00134	-0.01714	70	Data entry keyers
0.01131	0.01636	0.00000	71	Other administrative support

Private household occupations

0.00026	0.00045	0.00002	72	Private household occupations

Protective service occupations

0.01064	0.01617	-0.01002	73	Guards
-0.00008	-0.00007	-0.00013	74	Other protective services

Service occupations except household and protective services

0.00639	0.00917	-0.00095	75	Food service occupations
0.00059	0.00072	-0.00018	76	Health service occupations
0.00595	0.00941	-0.00835	77	Cleaning service occupations
0.00431	0.00796	-0.00393	78	Personal service occupations

Farming, forestry and fishing occupations

0.07111	0.08473	0.04086	79	Farming, forestry & fishing

Table 3.2 (cont.)

Precision production, craft, and repair occupations

0.00722	0.01256	-0.00168	81	Auto mechanics
-0.03084	-0.02879	-0.09895	82	Industrial machinery repairers
0.01125	0.01507	-0.01186	83	Electronics repairers
0.00141	0.00500	-0.00933	84	Heating, A/C, refrig mechanics
0.00485	0.01378	-0.02687	85	Other mechanics/repairers
-0.02235	-0.01592	-0.08850	86	Supervisors, construction
-0.00385	0.00263	-0.01150	87	Carpenters
-0.01022	-0.00402	-0.03902	88	Electricians
-0.00284	0.00452	-0.01126	89	Painters
-0.01301	-0.00532	-0.02759	90	Plumbers
-0.00374	0.00174	-0.00835	91	Other construction trades
-0.38447	-0.18917	-0.20119	92	Extraction occupations
0.00909	-0.02143	-0.13675	94	Tool and die makers
0.03240	0.02802	-0.08450	95	Machinists
0.02102	0.02006	-0.03159	96	Sheet metal workers
0.02669	-0.00393	-0.11047	97	Other precision metal workers
-0.10808	-0.15265	-0.23400	98	Precision machine workers
0.00380	0.00297	-0.00503	99	Precision food prod workers

Table 3.2 (cont.)

-0.01778	0.01990	-0.07537	100	Precision inspectors
-0.02015	-0.00101	-0.03885	101	Plant/system operators
-0.00995	0.00445	-0.07129	102	Other precision production operators

Machine operators, assemblers, and inspectors

0.00678	-0.01539	-0.13496	103	Metal/plastics machine operators
0.02106	0.03179	-0.02284	104	Fabricating machine operators
-0.07577	-0.07104	-0.19254	105	Plastic/wood machine operators
0.00220	0.00517	-0.04088	106	Printing machine operators
-0.08775	-0.13472	-0.24974	107	Textile machine operators
-0.13221	-0.18350	-0.28494	108	Textile sewing machine operators
-0.00083	0.00026	-0.01028	109	Laundry/dry cleaning operators
-0.00120	0.00402	-0.04981	110	Packing machine operators
-0.06617	-0.07465	-0.18564	111	Furnace, kiln, oven operators
-0.05421	-0.06477	-0.14726	112	Other specified machine operators
-0.02140	-0.01074	-0.07792	113	Miscellaneous machine operators
-0.00435	0.00284	-0.08725	114	Welders/cutters
-0.06453	-0.10012	-0.19891	115	Solderers/brazers
-0.02466	-0.03933	-0.15455	116	Assemblers
-0.01452	-0.06387	-0.15023	117	Hand working occupations
-0.05111	-0.07038	-0.17515	119	Other production inspectors

Transportation and material moving occupations

0.02581	0.03845	-0.00095	120	Truck drivers
0.00257	0.00393	-0.00343	122	Other motor vehicle operators
0.20714	0.21898	0.12930	123	Rail/water trans occupations
-0.09089	-0.05538	-0.17722	125	Crane/hoist & winch operators
-0.02080	0.05432	-0.07148	126	Excavating/grading/dozer operators
-0.04371	-0.01742	-0.06816	127	Other material moving occupations

Handlers, equipment cleaners, helpers and laborers

-0.05265	-0.02208	-0.03105	129	Helpers, craft & production
-0.02935	-0.02777	-0.09388	131	Freight/material handlers
0.00471	0.00543	-0.00638	132	Garage/service station occupations
-0.03734	-0.05107	-0.13551	133	Hand packers/packagers
0.00148	0.00862	-0.03284	134	Laborers except construction

Table 3.3 is designed to summarize the information contained in Table 3.2 in a readily accessible form. This table clearly shows that white-collar occupations were essentially exported in 1977 and 1982, but that many blue-collar skills were imported.

TOTAL JOBS IN NET EXPORTS

Table 3.4 provides information on jobs in net exports, jobs in consumption, and on jobs in occupations with positive and negative net exports for each major occupational group in each of the three years considered here.

On balance, over all the occupations considered, trade contributed 77,249 jobs in 1977 and 485,685 in 1982. However, this positive contribution turned to a net deficit of 2,506,456 jobs in 1985. Overall, the change from about one-half million positive contribution in 1982 to a two and one-half million negative jobs effect in 1985 implies that trade changes cost the economy about three million jobs between 1982 and 1985.

Net exports of professionals, for example, increased from 22,000 jobs in 1977 to 65,000 in 1982, but fell to net imports of 75,000 jobs in 1985. Clerical workers followed a similar pattern, from net exports of 171,000 jobs in 1977 to 276,000 jobs in 1982, but with a negative value of 128,000 jobs in 1985. However, some major occupational groups retained positive net exports in 1985. Net exports for sales jobs were 116,000 in 1977, 148,000 in 1982, and 34,000 in 1985. Net exports of farm workers were 105,000 in 1977, 132,000 in 1982, and 69,000 in 1985.

For machine operators, the major occupational group with the lowest R values, net imports were 290,000 jobs in 1977, 398,000 in 1982, and 1,303,000 in 1985. By 1985, net imports for this group were over 1,300,000 jobs, which represented half of the 2,506,000 jobs net imported over all occupations.

Table 3.5 lists R values in 1977 for 7 groups of occupations aggregated from the 13 major occupational groups. The right-hand side of this table gives R values for the corresponding groups of occupations in 1967, as obtained from Sveikauskas (1983). (These comparisons are necessarily quite rough, since the definitions of the major occupational groups used in the 1970 *Census of Population* as utilized by

Table 3.3 Number of Occupations with Positive R Values
Positive/Total

Occupation	1977	1982	1985
Executive	8/9	8/9	1/9
Professional	13/20	19/20	4/20
Technical	8/10	10/10	0/10
Sales	4/4	4/4	4/4
Administrative support	18/19	18/19	14/19
Private Household	1/1	1/1	1/1
Protective Service	1/2	1/2	0/2
Other service	4/4	4/4	0/4
Precision production	10/21	12/21	0/21
Machine operators	3/16	5/16	0/16
Transport	3/6	4/6	5/6
Helpers, laborers, handlers	2/5	2/5	0/5
Farming	1/1	1/1	1/1

Sveikauskas (1983) are different from the definitions used in the 1980 *Census of Population* used in this book. The Census Bureau itself did not attempt to create a bridge between the old and new occupational definitions. Therefore, it should be stressed that the comparisons in Table 3.5 are only approximate.)

Nevertheless, it is worth noting that both in the data developed in this book and in the previous most comparable study, skills of farm workers were exported and had the highest R value. This parallel is especially noteworthy because the data used in this book for farmers excluded the self-employed, but Sveikauskas (1983) includes "farm managers and workers." Sales and clerical skills are also exported on net in this study in 1977 and in 1967.

It should come as no surprise that professionals have a higher rank in 1967 than in 1977, since in 1967, the United States was the undisputed world technological leader. By 1977, both Japan and West Germany were providing a serious technological challenge.

The difference in R values between craftsmen, .00129, and precision production workers, -.01522, as well as between operatives (-.00165) and the combined machine operators and transportation and material moving category (-.02544) suggests the terms of trade may have turned against craftsmen and operatives between 1967 and 1977. Laborers' skills are imported on net in both years, but the previous study includes service workers with laborers. When data developed in this book for private household, protective service, and other service occupations are combined with data for laborers and handlers, the R value is mildly positive.

Several large caveats are in order. Most obviously the years are different. Sveikauskas' occupational data were based on the 1970 Census major groupings and the 1971 Survey of Occupational Employment, concorded to be compatible with the 1967 input-output table. The comparison in Table 3.5 is based on the 1977 data for this book. Moreover, the occupational classifications are different. Sveikauskas based this part of his work on 6 major occupational categories, whereas the finest level of occupational detail for this book is 13 groupings. As mentioned above, the occupational categories were changed between the 1970 and the 1980 Census. In addition, the *Survey of Occupational Employment* was in its pilot stage in 1971, and may have provided higher quality data in the 1982 Survey used in this book, since the sample is larger and since the Bureau of Labor Statistics had

Table 3.4 Net Export of Factor Services, Total of All 118 Occupations
and Thirteen Broad Occupational Groups, 1977, 1982, and 1985
(All figures are in numbers of jobs)

		1977	1982	1985
All 118 Occupations	Net Exports	77249	485685	-2506456
	Consumption	81628814	87674277	101295568
	Total Exports	689403	1072220	130212
	Total Imports	-612154	-586535	-2636668
Executive	Net Exports	40212	106820	-134791
	Consumption	8149653	8820985	10255416
	Total Exports	40232	106831	0
	Total Imports	-20	-11	-134791
Professional	Net Exports	21816	65471	-75372
	Consumption	10388293	11674143	12777897
	Total Exports	43244	71981	5493
	Total Imports	-21428	-6510	-80864
Technical	Net Exports	20187	50599	-52625
	Consumption	3198155	3617750	4132156
	Total Exports	27493	50599	0
	Total Imports	-7305	0	-52625
Sales	Net Exports	115587	147979	33509
	Consumption	6352480	6933012	8188614
	Total Exports	115587	147979	13509
	Total Imports	0	0	0
Clerical	Net Exports	170774	276214	-127709
	Consumption	15072443	16512764	19007236
	Total Exports	173217	277589	4618
	Total Imports	-2443	-1376	-132327
Private Household	Net Exports	301	475	24
	Consumption	1159368	1045990	1260858
	Total Exports	301	475	24
	Total Imports	0	0	0
Protective Services	Net Exports	7097	12052	-8809
	Consumption	1938953	2144060	2307601
	Total Exports	7195	12151	0

	Total Imports	-98	-100	-8809
Other Services	Net Exports	55134	93164	-38394
	Consumption	10478993	11790488	13201653
	Total Exports	55134	93164	0
	Total Imports	0	0	-38394
Farm, Forestry, Fisheries	Net Exports	105063	132239	69221
	Consumption	1477561	1560690	1694275
	Total Exports	105063	132239	69221
	Total Imports	0	0	0
Precision, Craft, Repair	Net Exports	-141409	-49431	-576276
	Consumption	9288934	9456584	11376826
	Total Exports	40747	61772	0
	Total Imports	-182156	-111203	-576276
Machine Operators	Net Exports	-290138	-397667	-1303447
	Consumption	7041424	6965928	8671916
	Total Exports	7607	5077	0
	Total Imports	-297745	-402744	-1303447
Transport, Material Moving	Net Exports	25355	75426	-64314
	Consumption	3366840	3387944	3957639
	Total Exports	69261	93991	17348
	Total Imports	-43906	-18565	-81661
Helpers, Laborers	Net Exports	-52730	-27656	-227474
	Consumption	3715716	3763937	4463482
	Total Exports	4322	18371	0
	Total Imports	-57052	-46027	-227474

Table 3.5 Comparison of R Values with Previous Literature

This book, for 1977			Sveikauskas (1983), for 1967	
R Value	Occupation	Rank	(X-M)/C	Occupation
.07111	Farmers	1	.01806	Farmers
.01337	Sales/clerical	2	.00857	Professional
.00378	Professional	3	.00251	Sales
.00057	Helpers, Laborers, Service	4	.00129	Craftsmen
-.01522	Precision prd.	5	-.00165	Operatives
.02544	Machine ops.	6	-.03303	Laborers, Service

probably refined and improved its data collection procedures. Finally, the previous study relies on the 1967 total requirements input-output table and calculations for this book are based on the 1977 input-output table. Undoubtedly this change in technology has also affected the results.

CHANGES IN TRADE AND JOB LOSS

The preceding section has examined the effect of the level of trade on jobs. However, from a certain perspective, the present labor market already reflects the job displacement associated with the current level of trade. From such a vantage point, changes in the number of jobs lost to trade for each occupation are the key measure of labor force disruption associated with trade.

Appendix Table 3.2 lists total job losses associated with trade for each of the 118 occupations between 1977-1982 and 1982-1985. As the numbers show, almost every occupation gained jobs from trade between 1977 and 1982. Every single one of the 118 occupations in fact lost jobs to trade between 1982 and 1985.

Although most occupations gained jobs from trade between 1977 and 1982, 17 of the occupations lost a total of 151,120 jobs to trade between these years. All the other occupations gained from trade between these years. All occupations lost jobs to trade between 1982 and 1985.

As might be expected because most of the estimates for the individual occupations are positive in the first period and negative in the second time span, the pattern of job gains and losses due to trade is broadly similar for the total labor force and for the thirteen major occupational groups. As Table 3.6 shows, trade contributed a net contribution of 404,942 new jobs in 1977-1982. Since 151,120 jobs were lost to trade over this same period at the detailed occupational level total job gains associated with change in trade between 1977 and 1982 were 404,942 + 151,120, or approximately 550,000 jobs. As Table 3.6 shows at the major occupational level, the total 1977-1982 effects of trade were negative for only the machinery operators category. If only data for the 13 categories are analyzed, 1977-1982 total job gains are 404,942 + 107,529, or approximately 510,000 jobs.

Table 3.6 Job Gains and Losses Due to Trade, Total Economy and
Thirteen Major Occupational Groups

1977-1982	1982-1985	Occupation
404942	-2941456	All Workers
66608	-241611	Executives
43655	-140845	Professionals
30412	-103225	Technical
34355	-142962	Sales
106921	-425361	Administrative support
173	-451	Private Household
4955	-20861	Protective Services
38031	-131559	Services
27176	-63018	Farming
88482	-476151	Precision Production
-107529	-905781	Machine Operators
50111	-140318	Transport Occupations
25087	-200007	Handlers

From 1982 to 1985 approximately 2,900,000 jobs were lost due to trade. Since the trade effect was negative for all 118 occupations between the years 1982 and 1985, the same results occur regardless of whether the full 118 occupational detail or the 13 major occupation groups are analyzed.

CHANGES IN THE STRUCTURE OF R PATTERNS

The figure on page 56 considers the relationship between R values for two different years. AA is a 45 degree line, with slope of 1, which passes through the origin, 0. At all points on this line the R value in the first year, on the horizontal axis, is equal to the R value in the second year, as shown on the vertical axis. Line BB represents a parallel 45 degree line in which R has declined the same absolute amount for each occupation. This case is represented by regression results where R_2 is a function of R_1, $R_2 = a + bR_1$, a is significantly negative, but b is still one. The line CC represents a situation in which R_2 declines more for occupations in which R has historically been relatively favorable. In this case, the coefficient b will be significantly less than one. Conversely, line DD represents a situation in which trade deterioration is minor for occupations in which the United States has historically had a strong trade situation, but deterioration is much worse for occupations in which the U.S. trade position is weak. In this case, b will be significantly greater than one.

Results explaining R in 1982 by R in 1977 are:

$$R_{1982} = .0049 + .808R_{1977}$$
$$n=118; R^2 =.79$$

Standard errors are .002 and .039 respectively. The t ratio for the null hypothesis that a=0 is 2.46 and that for the null hypothesis that B=1.0 is 4.89. Clearly, from 1977 to 1982, b is less than one and line CC is valid, which implies that jobs where the United States trade performance was strongest hurt most.

On the other hand, from 1982 to 1985 the relationship is:

$$R_{1985} = -.0417 + 1.1594R_{1982}$$

Based on the sample of 118 occupations, the t ratios were -13.02 and 2.29 respectively. The R^2 was .71.

In this case a is strongly negative, reflecting the overall deterioration of trade, but from 1982 to 1985 b is significantly greater

Figure.   Relationship Between R Values for Different Years

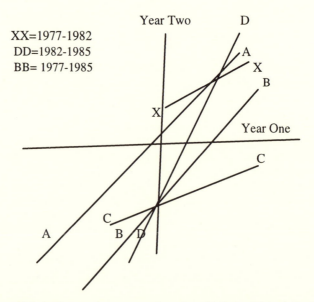

than one, which indicates that occupations in which the United States had an advantage did relatively well, but the real deterioration occurred in occupations in which U.S. R values were weak.

From 1977 to 1985 the relationship is as follows:

$$R_{1985} = -.0363 + .864R_{1977}$$

The t ratios were -8.45 and 1.60 respectively. The R^2 was .48.

Coefficient a is clearly negative, but the null hypothesis that b=1.0 cannot be rejected in a two-tailed test at the 95 percent level of significance, since the t ratio for this hypothesis fall in the range of +1.96 to -1.96. Therefore, over the total 1977 to 1985 period we cannot reject the hypothesis that the shift in R values was to a lower parallel line.

Thus, subperiod results show that b was less than one in 1977 to 1982, but greater than one in 1982 to 1985 when the trade deficit worsened dramatically. Furthermore, it is clear that different relationships occurred in the two subperiods, since R^2 for both the 1977 to 1982 and 1982 to 1985 periods was above .70, but R^2 for the total 1977 to 1985 period was less than .50. Therefore, from 1977 to 1982, jobs which historically had a strong trade position were hurt most, but from 1982 to 1985, deterioration occurred in occupations with the weakest trade position. For the period as a whole, the null hypothesis that net exports declined the same absolute amount for each occupation cannot be rejected.

MEASURES OF GOOD JOBS

Appendix Table 3.3 presents eight measures of how good a job each occupation represents for each of the 118 occupations considered in this book. Appendix Table 3.4 provides the same information for men. The attractiveness of each job is measured by earnings data for full-time workers in 1979, as obtained from the 1980 Census of Population. Each of the eight measures is divided by parallel earnings for similar categories of workers in the entire experienced labor force. Therefore, an income measure of 1.25 in Table A 3.3 indicates that workers in a particular category receive a twenty-five percent premium above all workers in the corresponding category in the entire labor force; conversely, an income measure of .90 shows that workers in another category earn only 90 percent of similar workers in the entire labor force.

Table 3.7 shows the ratio of earnings of officials and administrators in each educational category to earnings of all full-time workers in the same educational category. The first index of how good a job each occupation provides is obtained directly from the average hourly earnings of all full-time workers in that occupation. For officials and administrators, the first earnings index is 1.2856, which implies that officials and administrators on the average earn about 29 percent more than full-time workers in general.

The second index is earnings given educational category, which compares the earnings of personnel in a given occupation with earnings of their counterparts with similar educations in the total labor force. The index for officials and administrators is 1.1342 here, which implies that a typical worker in this occupation is paid 13 percent more than workers with similar educational backgrounds.

Measures three through eight provide similar measures of earnings given education for six specific educational attainment groups. Measure three refers to individuals with only an elementary school background, measure four to those with one to three years of high school, measure five to high school graduates, measure six to those with some college, measure seven to college graduates, and measure eight to those with some postgraduate education. Measure two is in fact a weighted index of measures three through eight, with the weights representing the proportion of the work force in each education category within each occupation.

For example, for officials and administrators, the first occupation, the relative earnings are 1.25 for those with an elementary school education, but only 1.05 for those with postgraduate education, suggesting that administration of this type is a better job for someone with less education. Similar patterns recur for other occupations and suggest that a good job is not necessarily the same for different portions of the work force. For example, computer programmers (occupation 43) provides good earnings for high school graduates (1.26) but poor earnings for college graduates (.92). The overall ranking for income given education (1.03) is close to average for this occupation. On the other hand, for lawyers (occupation 32) relative earnings are 1.23 for high school graduates, but 1.39 for graduate school; because most lawyers, as one might expect, have graduate degrees, relative earnings for the profession are also 1.39. For most blue-collar skills, jobs are much better for less educated groups; for example, welders (occupation 114), relative earnings are 1.12 for high school graduates but only .79 for college graduates. For the total occupation, earnings given education are 1.13.

Table 3.7 Illustrative Table for Officials and Administrators

Education Category	Earnings Ratio
Average Earnings	1.2856
Weighted Average Earnings	1.1342
Elementary School Graduates	1.2487
Some High School	1.2048
High School Graduates	1.1926
Some College	1.1758
College Graduates	1.0738
Graduate/Professional School	1.0457

RELATIONSHIPS BETWEEN JOB QUALITY MEASURES

The present section considers the relationships between the different earnings measures for the 118 occupations within the entire sample of occupations. Table 3.8 describes the relationships between the eight different concepts in the form of a matrix of R^2 between each of the different measures. The numbers in the table therefore show the proportion of explained variance if each measure is regressed against each alternative measure. The basic question examined is whether the various different measures of earnings do indeed provide additional information on the quality of jobs.

The explained variance between the average earnings index (measure 1) and average overall earnings given education (measure 2) is .70. Therefore, overall income explains about 70 percent of the variance in income given education. From another perspective, the income given education variable contains substantial information about job quality not contained in the average income data.

Income is in general more closely associated with income in each particular education class than with income given education. The relationships between overall income and income given education are particularly strong for education groups at the bottom and top of the educational distribution. R^2 is .87 for the relationship between overall income and income given education for the elementary school group. (Income given education for the elementary school group is of course equal to income for all workers within that educational category, subject to the use of a normalization factor which is the national wage for all workers with that educational attainment.) The corresponding R^2 is .88 for college graduates and for those with graduate education. R^2 between income in general and income for each of the other education groups is as follows: .76 for high school dropouts, .72 for high school graduates and .74 for college dropouts.

These same groups, the high school dropouts, high school graduates and college dropouts, have explained variation of .91, .90 and .87, respectively, between earnings measures for these groups and the overall index of earnings given education. This result is not surprising since workers in these groups are most heavily weighted in the overall workforce. (For example, high school graduates constituted 40.5 percent (23.6 million) of the 58.3 million full-time workers in 1980, persons who attended college another fifth (19.5 percent or 11.4 million) and high school dropouts one eighth (12.2 percent or 7.1 million). Also not surprisingly, earnings for any given education group is most highly correlated with earnings for the groups adjacent to it in education level.

Table 3.8. Matrix of R^2 Between Job Quality Variables

	YINC	Y/ED	Y1	Y2	Y3	Y4	Y5	Y6
YINC	1.00	.70	.87	.76	.72	.74	.88	.88
YED		1.00	.73	.91	.90	.87	.74	.59
Y1			1.00	.83	.72	.67	.76	.73
Y2				1.00	.90	.83	.74	.64
Y3					1.00	.96	.76	.60
Y4						1.00	.83	.66
Y5							1.00	.91
Y6								1.00

IV

Econometric Analysis

INTRODUCTION

This chapter analyzes the results of regressions relating jobs losses to net exports and earnings as formally stated in Chapter 1. Ordinary least squares regressions were performed in which the dependent variables were changes in the R values (number of jobs created by net exports/number of jobs created by consumption) for two subperiods: (1) 1977 to 1982 and (2) 1982 to 1985. Each of the eight earnings variables defined in Chapter 2 were entered as independent variables in separate equations. Additional regression analysis was performed in which the levels of the R values in each of the three years 1977, 1982, and 1985 were the dependent variables, and the same eight earnings measures were the independent variables.[1]

ANALYSIS OF DATA FOR MAJOR OCCUPATIONAL GROUPS

This subsection analyzes the relationship between net exports/consumption for each broad type of job and the quality of jobs within major occupational groups. There are 13 major occupational groups. This is the level of occupational detail at which all previous studies have approached the relationship between trade and jobs.

The first type of evidence to be examined is cross-section evidence. In this case, the relationship to be examined is

$$NX/C_i \text{ or } R_i = a + bJQ_i$$

R_i, the ratio of net exports to consumption for each occupation, is analyzed in terms of several facets of job quality for each occupation.

Table 4.1a presents cross-section results based upon this relationship for each of the eight different facets of job quality. The first line presents results measuring job quality by the average earnings of all workers. The second results measure job quality by the average earnings of workers given their educational attainments. The other rows report results in which the index of job quality is the earnings of workers in a particular educational group, relative to all workers in the nation with that same educational attainment.

The results in Table 4.1 consistently show no sign at all of a relationship between the effects of international trade and measures of job quality. For example, in 1977 the coefficient for average earnings of full-time workers is - .015, with a t ratio of -0.59. Better jobs have a slightly weaker trade performance, but the coefficient is not significantly different from zero. None of the coefficients in the upper portion of Table 4.1 is significant. On the basis of this evidence, we cannot conclude that there is any relationship between job quality and trade performance, although negative coefficients seem to predominate, which suggests, if anything, that better jobs are adversely affected by trade.

The latter portions of Table 4.1(b) analyze the change in R between 1977 and 1982 and between 1982 and 1985 in terms of these same eight measures of occupational job quality. The dependent variables are $R_{1982}-R_{1977}$ and $R_{1985}-R_{1982}$. There is also no relationship between changes in trade performance and job quality. From 1977 to 1982 most of the coefficients are positive, in that occupations characterized by high job quality have slightly better trade performance. (Net exports divided by consumption is greater in 1982 than in 1977.) Conversely, the coefficients tend to be negative in 1982 to 1985, implying that better jobs have worse trade performance in 1982 to 1985. However, in both of these time periods, the coefficients are never anywhere close to statistically significant. On the basis of this evidence, we cannot reject the hypothesis that there is absolutely no relationship between job quality and changes in trade performance.

Both the regressions, which study the cross-section relationship between trade performance and job quality, and the time-series regressions, which analyze the changes in trade performance as a function of job quality, show absolutely no effect for job quality. On the basis of this evidence, which is the level of occupational aggregation followed in all previous studies of the relationship between labor quality and trade, one would have to conclude that job quality is unrelated to trade performance.

Table 4.1a. Regression Results for 13 Occupational Groups

Earnings group	1977	1982	1985
Average			
earnings	-.015	-.012	-.015
T Ratios	-.587	-.379	-.331
Constant	.018	.020	-.007
R2	.11	.09	.09
Weighted	-.032	-.028	-.060
Earnings	-1.027	-.709	-.331
Constant	.034	.035	.034
R2	.16	.11	.16
Elementary	-.028	-.022	-.047
Graduates	-.981	-.642	-.929
Constant	.032	.031	.026
R2	.15	.11	.14
High School	-.027	-.021	-.052
Dropouts	-.901	-.568	-.957
Constant	.031	.030	.029
R2	.14	.10	.15
High School	-.029	-.025	-.050
Graduates	-1.000	-.692	-.942
Constant	.032	.033	.027
R2	.15	.12	.15
College	-.025	-.021	-.043
Dropouts	-.812	.565	-.776
Constant	.027	.028	.018
R2	.030	.10	.13
College	-.015	-.010	-.017
Graduates	-.439	-.241	-.278
Constant	.016	.017	-.007
R2	.09	.08	.08
Graduate school	-.009	-.005	-.000
	-.292	-.125	.007
Constant	.011	.013	-.021
R2	.08	.08	.08

Table 4.1b Regression Results for 13 Occupational Groups

Earnings Group	1977-1982	1982-1985
Average Earnings	.003	-.004
T Ratios	.403	-.143
Constant	.002	-.027
R2	.09	.08
Weighted Earnings	.005	-.032
	.466	-1.075
Constant	.000	-.032
R2	.09	.16
Elementary Graduates	.005	-.025
	.595	-.923
Constant	-.000	-.025
R2	.11	.140
High School Dropouts	.006	-.031
	.638	-1.076
Constant	-.001	-.001
R2	.11	.16
High School Graduates	.004	-.025
	.455	-.881
Constant	.001	-.006
R2	.09	.13
College Dropouts	.004	-.022
	.376	-.737
Constant	.002	-.011
R2	.09	.12
College Graduates	.005	-.007
	.479	.218
Constant	.001	-.024
	.10	.08
Graduate School	.004	-.005
	.466	-.172
Constant	.001	-.034
R2	.09	.08

However, thirteen occupational categories do not really provide a sufficiently large sample to study these issues. Because the relationship between trade and job quality is potentially a matter of considerable importance, it is useful to have a more comprehensive and larger sample. This book provides the information necessary to analyze this question with the greater information contained in a more detailed breakdown of occupational employment.

All the regressions above were also performed using R values and earnings measures for the 118 occupations. The next subsection of this chapter presents these results.

DATA ANALYSIS FOR DETAILED OCCUPATIONAL GROUPS

Table 4.2 summarizes the regression results for the 118 occupation analyses for both sexes, and Table 4.3 the comparable regression results for men. A fairly consistent picture emerges for both groups. First, in the 1977 to 1982 subperiod, years of more moderate trade deficits, when trade was more in equilibrium, trade was creating good jobs, in the sense that net exports/consumption increased for jobs in which earnings were typically high. The relationship between the change in the net export to consumption ratio and earnings given education was positive and significant for all education groups and for both of the alternative measures of overall earnings for both men and women and for men alone.

The coefficients in Table 4.2 are to be interpreted as follows. A coefficient of .016, which is the coefficient for the average earnings equation in the 1977-1982 study period for both sexes, means each 100-percent increase in average earnings is associated with a 1.6 percent increase in R, the share of jobs created by exports in relation to domestic consumption over this period. For the entire sample of both men and woman, these coefficients ranged from .016 to .033; for all groups whose educational attainment exceed elementary school, the coefficients ranged from .024 to .033. The R^2 indicates that each single independent variable by itself explains about 6 to 11 percent of the variance in changes in net exports. Moreover, the higher the educational level, the higher the coefficient, a pattern which also holds for men and in some of the cross-section results. This implies that changes in trade between 1977 and 1982 created the best jobs for workers in the highest education categories. The male coefficients over this study subperiod were slightly lower than for both sexes.

Table 4.2a Regression Results, 118 Occupations, Both Sexes

Earnings Group	1977-1982	1982-1985
Average Earnings	.016	.000
T Ratios	.027	.012
Constant	-.009	-.042
R2	.06	.01
Weighted Earnings	.027	-.039
	2.997*	-2.783*
Constant	-.022	-.003
R2	.08	.07
Elementary Graduates	.016	-.010
	2.604*	-1.066
Constant	-.013	-.029
R2	.06	.02
High School Dropouts	.024	.026
	2.928*	-2.075*
Constant	-.019	-.014
R2	.08	.04
High School Graduates	.025	-.031
	3.011*	-2.421*
Constant	-.020	-.009
R2	.08	.06
College Dropouts	.027	-.026
	3.093*	-1.892
Constant	-.021	-.016
R2	.08	.04
College Graduates	.033	-.033
	3.642*	-1.842
Constant	-.022	-.039
R2	.11	.01
Graduate School	.033	.015
	3.551*	1.059
Constant	-.019	-.053
R2	.11	.02

Table 4.2b. Regression Results, 118 Occupations, Both Sexes

Earnings Group	1977	1982	1985
Average		.018	.033
	.033		
Earnings	1.266	2.664*	1.909
Constant	-.021	-.031	-.073
R2	.02	.07	.04
Weighted	.009	.036	-.002
Earnings	.433	1.976*	-.088
Constant	-.013	-.034	-.037
R2	.01	.04	.01
Elementary	.012	.029	.019
Graduates	.895	2.318*	1.057
Constant	-.018	-.031	.061
R2	.02	.05	.02
High School	.018	.042	.016
Dropouts	1.010	2.615*	.711
Constant	-.023	-.043	-.057
R2	.02	.06	.01
High School	.020	.044	.014
Graduates	1.070	2.726*	.604
Constant	-.024	-.044	-.054
R2	.02	.07	.01
College	.021	.048	.022
Dropouts	1.057	2.752*	.900
Constant	-.024	-.045	-.061
R2	.02	.07	.02
College	.017	.050	.048
Graduates	.824	2.740*	1.848
Constant	-.018	-.039	-.079
R2			
Graduate School	.017	.049	.065
	.795	2.663*	2.524*
Constant	-.016	-.034	-.087
R2	.02	.07	.06

However, there is evidence that this positive association between relatively high-paying jobs and exports was reversed when the overall trade deficit mushroomed. In the 1982 to 1985 period, the only significant variable both in the equations for both sexes and in the equations for men alone were negative. This result is seen more strongly in the equations for both sexes: the b coefficients were negative and significant in three of the eight equations. The coefficient in the equation for high school dropouts was -.026 and in the equation for high school graduates it was -.031; both were significant. The weighted earnings variable, which was also significant, was -.039. Thus, we can conclude that over 1982 to 1985, trade changes did not continue to create good jobs; at best they had a neutral impact, at worst they, in fact, even destroyed good jobs for high school dropouts and high school graduates, two groups for which concern over labor market success is often expressed. Moreover, the coefficients for two of the remaining four education groups, for college dropouts and college graduates were negative and almost significant, but their t ratios of 1.89 and -1.84 did not meet the 95 percent two-tail level of -1.96. It should also be noted that these relationships were sufficient to influence the overall weighted earnings measure, which was also negative and significant. Generally, however, most of the relationships between changes in R and job quality were not significant over the 1982-1985 period, so we can conclude that trade did not significantly increase or decrease the quality of jobs for most education groups but had a neutral effect. In the equations for men, again the only significant variable was negative, the weighted average earnings ratio.

In terms of the cross-section results in Tables 4.2, in the equations for 1982, coefficients were all positive and significant for both sexes and for seven of the eight equations for men. The coefficients for men were generally higher than for both sexes, as follows: average earnings, .033 for both sexes, .039 for men; average weighted earnings, .036 for both sexes, not significant for men; elementary school graduates, .029 for both sexes and for men; high school dropouts, .042 and .049; high school graduates, .044 and .054; college dropouts, .048 and .056; college graduates, .050 and .052; graduate school attendees, .049 and .046. Again the results repeat the general pattern found in the time series analysis of increasing as the level of educational attainment increases up until graduate school.

In the 1985 sets of equations, in the equations for men, the average earnings ratio was positive and significant, indicating net benefits from trade. However, in the both sexes set of equation, the benefits of trade were not apparent except for the highly educated. In the both sexes equations, although all coefficients were positive, none were significant, except for persons who had attended graduate school. For men, in addition to the positive significant relationship between net exports and the average earnings ratio reported above, male college graduates and men who attended graduate school also obtained benefits from trade. The coefficients were .065 and .074 respectively. The coefficients for the 1977 cross-section were all positive but, disappointingly, none were significant. Despite the evidence from the 1982 and 1985 cross-sections that the level of trade contributes to the quality of jobs, the evidence from the 1977 cross-section is much weaker. Consequently, we cannot conclude unambiguously that, as a general case, trade is associated with a better quality of jobs.

In summary, during the early years of the study period, 1977 to 1982, the change in the ratio of net exports to consumption was associated with better jobs, as the set of positive, significant coefficients in Tables 4.2 and 4.3 indicates. Moreover, the higher the educational level, the higher the positive coefficient. However, in the 1982-1985 period, when the nation began to run up tremendous trade deficits, the relationship between the change in jobs gained due to net exports to jobs gained due to consumption ratio and good jobs disappeared. In this set of equations, the only significant coefficients, for high school dropouts and high school graduates, and the weighted average earnings ratio variable, were actually negative in the both sexes equation. For men only, the overall weighted coefficient was significant, and it, too, was negative.

In the 1982 cross-section results, trade was also associated with good jobs, and again, the higher the education level, the higher the positive coefficient. By 1985, for men, overall trade had a positive influence on good jobs, but in terms of the specific education groups, the net benefit of trade was apparent only for men with at least a college degree, or for both sexes in only one group, those who had graduate school education.

The empirical results show that when the data for net exports and earnings and earnings given education are aggregated to the 13 broad Census occupational groups, there is no relationship between net trade performance and job quality for average earnings, overall job quality, or job quality for any of the six education groups. This conclusion holds for the 1977 to 1982 and 1982 to 1985 periods and also for the 1977, 1982, and 1985 cross-sections.

Table 4.3a. Regression Results for Men, 118 Occupations

Earnings Groups	1977-1982	1982-1985
Average Earnings	.015	.009
	(1.985)*	(.752)
Constant	-.009	-.050
R2	.04	.01
Weighted Earnings	.029	-.044
	(2.451)*	(-2.440)*
Constant	-.022	-.000
R2	.06	.06
Elementary Graduates	.014	-.006
	(2.056)*	(-.062)
Constant	-.010	-.034
R2	.04	.01
High School Dropouts	.021	-.022
	(2.168)*	(-1.503)
Constant	-.016	-.019
R2	.05	.03
High School Graduates	.023	-.018
	(2.248)*	(-1.190)
Constant	-.017	-.023
R2	.05	.02
College Dropouts	.027	-.013
	(2.516)*	(-.814)
Constant	-.019	-.029
R2	.06	.01
College Graduates	.032	.013
	(3.030)*	(.783)
Constant	-.020	-.052
R2	.08	.01
Graduate School	.031	.028
	(2.931)*	(1.742)
Constant	-.017	-.062
R2	.08	.03

Table 4.3b Regression Results for Men, 118 Occupations, Cross-section

Earnings Group	1977	1982	1985
Average	.024	.039	.048
Earnings	(1.475)	(2.653)*	(2.335)*
Constant	.027	-.036	-.085
R2	.03	.07	.05
Weighted	.012	.042	-.002
Earnings	(.474)	(1.758)	(-.064)
Constant	-.016	-.038	-.038
R2	.01	.03	.01
Elementary	.015	.029	.022
Graduates	(.998)	(-2.160)*	(1.198)
Constant	-.021	-.031	-.065
R2	.02	.05	.02
High School	.028	.049	.027
Dropouts	(1.349)	(2.623)*	(1.025)
Constant	-.033	-.049	-.068
R2	.02	.06	.02
High School	.309	.054	.035
Graduates	(1.407)	(2.743)*	(1.271)
Constant	-.035	-.052	-.075
R2	.03	.07	.02
College	.029	.056	.043
Dropouts	(1.259)	(2.700)*	(1.458)
Constant	-.031	-.040	-.079
R2	.02	.07	.03
College	.020	.052	.065
Graduates	(.832)	(2.445)*	(2.213)*
Constant	-.020	-.040	-.092
R2	.01	.06	.05
Graduate School	.015	.046	.074
	(1.591)	(2.599)	(2.591)*
Constant	-.015	-.032	-.094
R2	.01	.05	.06

Because economic theory does suggest any specific functional form for the relationship between the R values and the different measures of job quality, it is possible that the relationship between these variables may not be linear. This possibility was examined by tests conducted to determine whether the relationships might be curvilinear. In these tests, a squared independent variable was added to the linear independent variables so far examined. These tests were conducted for six measures of trade performance: levels of trade in 1977, 1982, and 1985, and changes in the R values for 1977 to 1982, 1982 to 1985, and 1977 to 1985. Five measures of job quality were selected for examination with each of these six measures of trade: the overall income, overall income given education, elementary school, high school, and college graduate measures of job quality.

However, of these thirty squared terms estimated for each of the five types of job quality and each of the six time periods, the squared term was significantly different from zero at the 95 percent level in only one case. The only case in which the squared term was influential was the 1977 to 1982 change for elementary school graduates, which is insignificant on the second part of Table 4.1. However, with a squared term the relationship is as follows:

$$R= .019 \quad -.087(YGED1) \quad +.027(YGED1)^2$$

T ratios are .79, -2.45, and 2.24 respectively. R^2 is .06.

The pattern of results reported in this chapter indicates that the detailed occupational information which is at the heart of this book has made a difference. If analysis is conducted at the level of major occupational groups, which is how all prior studies have approached the question of the relationship between trade and labor quality, no distinct patterns emerge. The greater detail used in this book generates a definite pattern of meaningful results and hence provides a more conclusive view of the relationship between trade and good jobs.

RELATIONSHIP AMONG JOB QUALITY VARIABLES

The econometric results reported above raise the question of the appropriate relationship between variables 3 through 8, which measure a job's quality for each of the six educational groups (by dividing earnings of full-time workers in that educational group in that occupation by the earnings of all full-time workers in the same educational category), and variable 2, which is a weighted measure of variables 3 through 8, with the weights representing the proportion of full-time workers in each of the six educational categories in that occupation. The central issue here is why average earnings is closer to average earnings given education for each education group than to the overall index of earnings given education, weighted by the proportion of workers in each education group. We now explore the labor market behavior patterns which account for these results.

The link between these concepts is provided by Taubman and Wales (1973), who show that workers with high amounts of educational attainment are able to enter occupations in which the returns for their personal characteristics are high, or, in other words, the better jobs. On the other hand, less educated workers are not able to enter those occupations where the returns to their personal characteristics are high; instead, they are shunted to the end of the job queue and forced to take jobs where earnings are lower, the bad jobs. The screening or queuing hypothesis, which makes average educational attainment in a job vary with its level of wages, causes average earnings in an occupation to vary quite strongly with earnings given education measures.

Consistent with the Taubman-Wales argument, the earnings data show that most of the workers are typically in very highly educated groups for occupations such as electrical engineers, health diagnosing occupations and lawyers in which earnings are higher than average for all educational groups. Conversely, in occupations with consistently poor relative earnings, such as food service workers, most of the workers are clustered in very low education groups.

Table 4.4 illustrates how the Taubman-Wales findings appear in the data used for this book. The independent variable is earnings in the occupation for the education group relative to economywide earnings for the education group. The dependent variable is the proportion of workers in the occupation in the education group. Separate regressions are run within each of the six education groups. The first regression in Table 4.4 deals with workers with graduate school degrees. For lawyers, for example, earnings for graduate degree holders have a relative value of 1.39 and 90 percent of all lawyers are in this highest education group. For postal clerks, relative earnings for a graduate degree are .67 and only 2 percent of postal clerks fall into this educational classification. The regression equation indicates that these examples are typical. Graduate workers account for a large share of an occupation's workers when relative wages for graduates are high in this occupation.

Similarly, for workers with an elementary school education, work as a tool and die maker provides a relatively good income (1.46); however, only 7 percent of tool and die workers have an elementary school education. In contrast, food service work is poorly paid for such workers (.65), yet 17 percent of all food service workers have only an elementary education. As the last regression in Table 4.4 shows, this relationship is also typical in the sense that uneducated workers cluster in those occupations where pay for uneducated workers is least. More generally, the coefficients in Table 4.4 are positive and significant for the three groups with the highest educational attainment and negative and significant for the three least educated groups of workers. For these categories, the proportion of workers across occupations with graduate training, college degrees, or some college training is positively related to relative return. Workers with these levels of education are able to take advantage of high relative earnings by flocking to occupations where the returns are high. Moreover, the pattern of increasing coefficients indicates this process is especially pronounced as the level of educational attainment increases. Conversely, relative earnings is negatively related to the proportion of the work force with a given education in an occupation for those with less education, high school graduates, some high school, and elementary school graduates. The turning point from a positive supply response to negative association implying occupational crowding effects thus occurs between high school graduates and college attendance, which is also a rough indicator of social class within the society at large, implying that perhaps social mobility is associated in part with the presence of economic options.

The high R^2's underscore the significance of these results: relative earnings explain more than one-third of the variance in the proportion of workers with graduate training and college degrees and 6 percent for those with some college. For the half of the categories with less formal schooling, R^2 ranges from 13 to 18 percent.

It should be noted that these results are also consistent with a model of unmeasured ability or motivation that affects both the number of years of schooling and the choice of occupation. Taubman and Wales considered a wide variety of individual characteristics with micro data and still concluded that the evidence supported a screening explanation of income differences. As always, however, unmeasured variables could account for the patterns observed.

Table 4.4 Percentage of Workers as a Function of Relative Earnings for
118 Occupations, 1980

Level of Education	Coefficient	R2
Graduate School	.507 (8.280)	.37
College Graduate	.289 (8.056)*	.36
Some College	.092 (2.538)*	.06
High School Graduate	-.218 (-3.940)*	.13
Some High School	-.126 (-4.339)*	.14
Elementary School	-1.05 (-4.979)*	.18

Because of these systematic differences between occupations in the weights of different educational categories, the overall weighted index of job quality (variable 2) tends to be quite different from its components (variables 3 through 8). In Table 4.2a, in the 1977 to 1982 period, the time span for which all coefficients were positive and significant, the coefficient for the weighted earnings measure, .027, indeed lies between the coefficient for elementary school graduates of .016 and that for persons who attended graduate school of .033. However, in the 1982-1985 time period, the coefficient for the weighted earnings measure at -.039 is certainly not within the range of the other significant coefficients: -.026 for high school dropouts and negative .030 for high school graduates.

In the cross-section results for 1982 reported in Table 4.2a, which were all positive and significant, the .036 coefficient for the weighted earnings measure is indeed in the range of the .029 for elementary school graduates and the .050 for college graduates. In this Table, none of the 1977 coefficients were significant and hence will not be analyzed, nor were most of the 1985 coefficients, including the weighted average coefficient in question.

For the men only sets of equations (Table 4.3), in the 1977-1982 subperiod, the weighted average coefficient falls nicely within the range, but in the 1982-1985 period, it is the only significant variable. In the 1982 equations (Table 4.3b), the coefficient of the weighted average variable is the only insignificant variable, with a t ratio of 1.758.

NOTES

1. Early versions of this book defined good jobs by the presence of high wages in the total work force, including both men and women full-time workers. Some readers of this early formulation commented that it looked as though good jobs, so defined, were primarily those in which men predominated, whereas poor jobs were those with many women. Because this is a reasonable interpretation, the total set of calculations was conducted once more defining the presence of good jobs solely by the pay of full-time male workers. However, the basic patterns and conclusions from this reanalysis were broadly similar to those reached from the evidence on the total full-time work force. Therefore, the discussion of good jobs does not appear to rest solely on differences in compensation between men and women workers.

V

Conclusions

This chapter attempts to pull together the various strands of evidence from the prior discussion and put them together in a cohesive overview. However, certain portions of the evidence do not fit the broad pattern of the remaining evidence very well. Therefore, the conclusions drawn here are tentative.

The main evidence shows quite clearly that over the 1977 to 1982 period trade on balance created good jobs for American workers within every educational category. In 1977, the U.S. merchandise trade deficit was $37 billion; in 1982 the corresponding deficit was $38 billion. Therefore, 1977-1982 represents a period in which the trade deficit was very stable, and even decreased in real terms. The 1977-1982 results therefore show the effects of trade on U.S. jobs in a normal period, when the normal effect of trade can be evaluated. Over this normal time period, trade provided good jobs for all educational categories of U.S. workers.

However, from 1982 to 1985, trade clearly destroyed good jobs for U.S. workers in most educational categories. From 1982 to 1985, the U.S. trade deficit increased from $38 billion to $134 billion, as Reaganomics and the associated high dollar destroyed U.S. jobs in many sectors in which the United States normally has a comparative advantage. It is certainly tempting to interpret this as a disequilibrium phenomenon; if trade destroys jobs in normally strong industries, many good jobs can be destroyed.

It must be noted, however, that the analysis of trade levels for 1977, 1982, and 1985, as compared to the 1977-1982 and 1982-1985 changes does not fully support this interpretation. It is certainly true that trade on balance created new jobs in 1982, as the above scenario would suggest, and that trade no longer created good jobs in 1985, as the effect of the disastrous fiscal and monetary policy in the United States was seen in the numbers.

However, in the above interpretation one would expect trade to be associated with good jobs in 1977, as the effect of years of relatively free trade was reflected in the figures. One would expect a positive strong effect in the analysis of the 1977 level of trade figures. Instead, in 1977 trade does not seem to be associated with good jobs at all; there is no sign of any positive effect or negative effect.

One possibility is that the trade figures in 1977 already reflected a disequilibrium position and a deterioration of trade. For example, the merchandise trade balance was actually a surplus of $3 billion in 1975, and a deficit of $16 billion in 1976. This deteriorated to a deficit of $37 billion in 1977. Perhaps this decline already destroyed many of the good jobs created by trade, such as occurred later in the 1982-1985 period, when many good jobs were destroyed by trade. Still, the 1975-1977 trade deterioration of $40 billion was modest by the standards of later years. It seems unlikely that such a relatively slight shift in the trade balance could offset the effect of many years of equilibrium trade which can have been expected to create many good jobs, on the basis of the 1977-1982 evidence. Therefore, the analysis offered above must be tempered by the acknowledgment that the 1977 evidence does not fit together closely to suggest the overall interpretation discussed here can be any more than a somewhat tentative explanation.

The methodology used in this book can be used to evaluate the effects of the net trade balance on job gains and losses for any country that has data similar to the data described herein. Webster (1993) used a similar method to estimate the factor content of trade in Great Britain. In addition, an analyst may modify this methodology to determine the effects of trade in terms of either exports and/or imports separately to assess whether increased imports, for example, or declining export performance, are associated with job losses.

Another application of the methodology described above has been to determine bilateral trade flows. Maskus, Sveikauskas and Webster (1994) studied US/UK trade flows using the methodology and data sources developed in this book. However, none of the studies cited linked trade with job quality data, a key innovation introduced herein.

Appendix

Table A3.1 presents the first essential information for this book. In each line, the first number represents the export or import of labor services, the second item jobs generated by domestic consumption, the third item the ratio of net exports to consumption, which this book refers to as R. Each of these items is measured in number of jobs. There are three lines for each occupation, one line for the given occupation for 1977, one line for the occupation for 1982, and one line for the occupation for 1985. The occupational title is listed at the end of these three lines, as is the occupation number as appears in the *Earnings by Occupation* volume of the 1980 *Census of Population*. The remaining tables contained in this appendix are discussed in the main text of this book.

Table A3.1 Net Exports, Consumption, and Exports/Consumption,
1977, 1982, and 1985

[All figures are in number of jobs]
Note: There are three lines for each occupation; the first is NX, C, R for
1977; the second NX, C, and R fo3

NX	C	Ratio	Occupation
.0	177121.2	.00000	OFFICIALS
.0	195322.7	.00000	ADMINIST
.0	203003.0	.00000	1
-20.0	151359.3	-.00013	ADMINIST,
-10.8	166639.3	-.00006	EDUCATION
-83.6	175856.7	-.00047	4
214.9	20777.7	.01034	OTHER SP
335.0	23381.0	.01433	MGRS
-377.3	27940.9	-.01350	6
22136.0	5966197.0	.00371	MGR, NEC
72310.0	6443329.0	.01122	SALARIED
-106983.9	7535444.0	-.01412	7
3412.3	595793.3	.00573	ACCOUNTANTS,
13204.4	638283.1	.02069	AUDITORS
-10116.7	744430.4	-.01358	9
256.0	270862.3	.00095	PERSONNEL
2347.1	299012.3	.00785	SPECIAL
-4642.8	336893.5	-.01378	10
6467.6	297416.6	.02175	BUYERS,
8672.3	321729.7	.02696	PURCH AGENTS
-3386.9	384462.4	-.00881	11
132.6	313119.9	.00042	
388.0	343395.9	.001130	INSPECTOR
-357.7	362812.2	-.00010	12
7612.7	357006.1	.02132	OTHER MGR
9574.5	389892.0	.02456	REL OCCUP
-8814.7	484572.9	-.01825	
2045.2	39847.3	.05133	
2670.3	44671.0	.05978	ARCHITECTS
1154.3	50562.9	.02283	14
2214.1	152237.8	.01454	
3569.9	164435.4	.02171	CIVIL ENG
314.3	181484.8	.00173	15
8354.4	239595.0	.03487	
13387.4	298032.7	.04492	ELEC ENG
-11021.1	400688.7	-.02751	16
163029.0	98430.6	.03077	

Table A3.1 (cont.)

NX	C	Ratio	Occupation
3466.1	107204.5	.03233	INDUS ENG
-8445.7	145078.1	-.05821	17
8129.2	169959.2	.0478	
720.5	178515.9	.04885	MECH ENG
-8545.2	226311.9	-.03776	18
-4635.5	318203.6	-.01457	
4362.1	336399.5	.01297	OTHER ENG
-19612.3	422634.9	-.0464	19
-205.6	29749.1	-.00691	
682.3	31677.6	.02154	SURVEYORS
-182.3	35660.2	-.00511	20
1518.2	224800.6	.00675	SYSTEMS
5199.1	247370.8	.02102	ANALYSTS
-4683.2	293510.7	-.01596	21
-228.4	46576.1	-.00490	
287.5	50741.3	.00567	MATHEMAT
-807.4	57430.9	-.01406	23
-518.7	73592.3	-.00705	
1184.0	76474.6	.01548	CHEMISTS
-3771.3	88173.3	-.04277	24
-15328.8	208344.8	-.07360	OTHER PHYS
-6510.1	223248.8	-.02916	SCIENTISTS
-11011.0	244019.8	-.04512	25
893.0	369338.7	.00241	HEALTH DIAG.
1099.1	440073.5	.00250	OCCUPATIONS
340.6	481216.3	.00071	26
890.2	1120806.0	.00079	REGISTER
1447.3	1361810.0	.00106	NURSES
-237.5	1456642.0	-.00016	27
191.4	357339.3	.00054	OTHER HEALTH
309.0	421666.0	.00073	OCCUPATIONS
-74.4	460802.8	-.00016	28
-304.4	3755597.0	-.00008	
256.8	4142165.0	.00006	TEACHERS
-3715.8	4388606.0	-.00085	29
-206.5	148676.9	-.00139	
479.7	166240.0	.00288	SOCIAL SCI
-455.2	179197.3	-.00254	30
674.9	453337.0	.00149	
1095.6	516079.4	.00212	SOCIAL WORK
-39.9	553539.0	.00007	31
6953.8	263140.0	.02643	
10120.2	289739.5	.03493	LAWYERS

Table A3.1 (cont.)

NX	C	Ratio	Occupation
3683.3	318590.9	.01156	3 2
7284.6	606304.9	.01201	WRITERS,
11627.8	677848.1	.01715	ARTISTS
-7536.0	773951.8	-.00974	3 3
1066.1	1712417.0	.00062	OTHER PROF.
2016.0	1899749.0	.00106	SPECIAL OCCUP.
-726.0	2019795.0	-.00036	3 4
795.4	475651.6	.00167	LICENSED
1185.5	578995.3`	.00205	NURSES
-84.2	629486.1	-.00013	3 5
196.8	565316.5	.00035	OTHER HEALTH
225.8	677715.6	.00033	TECHNICIANS
-1902.9	727901.5	-.00261	3 6
10688.4	268305.1	.03984	ELECTRONIC
16239.5	309953.8	.05239	TECHNICIANS
-3820.0	397021.5	-.00962	3 7
2114.6	56988.1	.03711	INDUSTRIAL
2324.3	62008.6	.03748	TECHNICIANS
-5451.5	82784.9	-.06585	3 8
4820.8	230460.6	.02092	DRAFTING
7965.7	241330.8	.03301	TECHNICIANS
-11321.9	297043.1	-.03812	3 9
-7008.4	445602.6	-.01573	OTHER SCI. AND
1268.2	476174.1	.00267	ENG. TECH.
-19938.2	545358.1	-.03656	4 0
-296.9	66722.3	-.00445	AIRPLANE
1502.6	66242.4	.02268	PILOTS
-2084.0	80737.1	-.02581	4 1
423.3	55841.5	.00758	
511.7	60989.3	.00839	CONTROLLER
-289.7	65809.4	-.00440	4 2
3025.7	230291.3	.01314	COMPUTER
7416.6	260129.0	.02851	PROGRAMMER
-5022.6	322882.1	-.01556	4 3
5427.8	802975.3	.00676	OTHER
11959.0	884211.6	.01353	TECHNICIANS
-2710.4	983131.8	-.00276	4 4
2626.9	359016.2	.00732	SALES, FINANCIAL
5147.3	390333.1	.01319	SERVICES
2357.7	446543.0	.00528	4 7
7212.1	1389840.0	.00519	
10614.3	1553319.0	.00683	CASHIERS

Table A3.1 (cont.)

NX	C	Ratio	Occupation
3226.5	1802887.0	.001790	49
17935.9	2059251.0	.00871	OTHER SALES
24019.0	2278149.0	.01054	RET, SERV
12883.7	2667902.0	.00483	50
87812.5	2544373.0	.03451	SALES
108198.8	2711211.0	.03991	OCCUPATIONS
15041.3	3271282.0	.00460	51
1319.0	232344.9	.00568	COMPUTER
4659.6	255518.5	.01824	OPERATOR
-3668.2	299727.6	-.01224	53
17580.0	2193354.0	.00803	
38003.6	2396677.0	.01586	SECRETARY
-27521.3	2744704.0	-.01003	54
8786.6	1078666.0	.00815	STENO,
14428.1	1192501.0	.01210	TYPISTS
-4270.1	1319495.0	-.00324	55
311.6	309050.9	.00101	
2673.4	350647.0	.00762	RECEPTIONISTS
-2488.8	396716.6	-.00627	56
3640.3	216775.8	.01679	OTHER INFO
7098.3	231667.6	.03064	CLERKS
239.2	279105.9	.00086	57
223.5	225484.1	.00099	FILE
2409.5	251990.5	.00956	CLERKS
-1865.2	284427.1	-.00656	58
9250.5	555355.8	.01666	OTHER REC
12943.5	607640.5	.02130	CLERKS
-3935.6	697210.1	-.00564	59
11555.8	1368333.0	.00845	ACCOUNT
23345.7	1473126.0	.01585	CLERKS
-17695.9	1715658.0	.01031	60
-2443.0	176055.8	-.01388	PAYROLL
-1375.5	185148.0	-.00743	CLERKS
-9166.1	216600.3	-.04232	61
7547.3	333558.3	.02263	OTH FINANCIAL
9336.6	370379.6	.02521	CLERKS
-.7	427403.6	-.00000	62
5010.8	315995.2	.01586	TELEPHONE
7666.5	362153.3	.02117	OPERATORS
-175.2	408121.9	-.00043	63
6425.5	595952.6	.01078	POST CLERKS
10276.4	667847.0	.01539	MAIL CARRIERS

Table A3.1 (cont.)

NX	C	Ratio	Occupation
-7869.2	788842.2	-.00998	64
2425.2	159844.4	.01517	PRODUCTION
2756.2	171405.0	.01608	COORDINATORS
-15029.9	220543.6	-.06815	65
11359.9	503996.3	.02254	SHIPPING
12361.3	521132.9	.02372	CLERKS
-23446.3	636667.3	-.03683	66
30766.6	1208660.0	.02546	STOCK, INV
37310.9	1310643.0	.02847	CLERKS
2347.1	1565298.0	.00150	67
380.4	414792.7	.00092	RECORDING
2007.4	445158.9	.00451	CLERKS
-9538.0	500940.5	-.01904	68
3282.7	395514.9	.00830	
4519.2	440780.8	.01025	INVESTIGTR
2003.8	493957.9	.00406	69
2124.2	260451.6	.00816	DATA ENTRY
4093.1	285386.8	.01434	KEYERS
-5656.6	330040.2	-.01714	70
51226.7	4528257.0	.01131	OTH ADMIN
81700.2	4992961.0	.01636	SUP OCCUP
27.8	5681776.0	.00000	71
301.1	1159368.0	.00026	PRIVATE
474.5	1045990.0	.000454	HH OCCUP
23.7	1260858.0	.00002	72
7195.2	676231.7	.01064	
12151.4	751647.0	.01617	GUARDS
-8620.6	860390.9	-.01002	73
-98.4	1262721.0	-.00008	OTR PROT
-99.5	1392413.0	-.00007	SERVICES
-188.1	1447210.0	-.00013	74
34074.3	5336140.0	.00639	FOOD SERV
54757.2	5970082.0	.00917	OCCUP
-6363.9	6688761.0	-.00095	75
797.8	1347486.0	.00059	HEALTH
1172.5	1625306.0	.00072	SERV OCC
-325.0	1801584.0	-.00018	76
14182.2	2384597.0	.00595	CLEANING SERV.
24952.1	2651625.0	.00941	OCCUP
-24906.7	2982652.0	-.00835	77
6080.0	1410770.0	.00431	PERSONAL SERV
12282.6	1543475.0	.00796	OCCUP

Table A3.1 (cont.)

NX	C	Ratio	Occupation
-6798.5	1728656.0	-.00393	78
105062.6	1477561.0	.07111	FARM, FORESTRY,
132238.5	1560690.0	.08473	FISH OCC
69220.8	1694275.0	.04086	79
5046.2	698708.4	.00722	AUTOMOBILE
9203.3	732746.6	.01256	MECHANICS
-1445.6	861095.2	-.00168	81
-11509.0	373212.3	-.03084	IND MACH
-10718.1	372236.6	-.02879	REPAIR
-43949.2	444133.4	-.09895	82
1376.1	122315.8	.01125	ELECTRONIC
2100.0	139323.2	.01507	REPAIR
-1831.4	154455.6	-.01186	83
175.7	124465.8	.00141	HEAT, AC,
623.7	124696.0	.00500	REFR MECH
-1386.1	148625.2	-.00933	84
9261.2	1910619.0	.00485	OTHER MECH
27655.3	2007248.0	.01378	+ REPAIR
-63067.9	2347040.0	-.02687	85
-25383.1	1135629.0	-.02235	SUPERVISORS
-18145.8	1139871.0	-.01592	CONSTRUCT
-123124.9	1391213.0	-.08850	86
-2084.8	541551.3	-.00385	
1378.8	523472.1	.00264	CARPENTER
-7333.8	637790.3	-.01150	87
-4711.4	461111.2	-.01022	
-1805.1	448531.8	-.00402	ELECTRICNS
-21340.5	546968.5	-.03902	88
-575.3	202673.7	-.00284	
911.8	201931.3	.00452	PAINTERS
-2704.1	240068.1	-.01126	89
-4744.2	364615.6	-.01301	
-1883.0	353709.6	-.00532	PLUMBERS
-11790.5	427285.4	-.02759	90
-3050.6	814785.1	-.00374	OTHER CON
1404.3	807573.2	.00174	TRADES
-7988.7	956465.5	-.00835	91
-98076.6	255094.6	-.38447	EXTRACT
-44645.6	236011.2	-.18917	OCCUPAT
-54579.9	271289.3	-.20119	92
1259.4	138489.6	.00909	TOOL, DIE
-2761.3	128857.1	-.02143	MAKERS

Table A3.1 (cont.)

NX	C	Ratio	Occupation
-23800.2	174044.6	-.13675	94
8882.4	274115.7	.03240	
7496.2	267568.8	.02802	MACHINIST
-28927.2	342319.7	-.08450	95
4128.2	196360.3	.02102	SHEET METAL
3805.4	189741.5	.02006	WORKERS
-7438.0	235425.6	-.03159	96
6498.2	243490.7	.02669	OTHER PRECS
-926.4	235949.8	-.00393	METAL WORK
-33095.5	299579.0	-.11047	97
-20582.8	190433.5	-.10808	PRECISION
-29979.9	196401.9	-.15265	MACH WORK
-53634.0	229203.2	-.23400	98
916.9	241265.2	.00380	PRECISION
759.9	255881.3	.00297	FOOD PROD
-1454.1	288856.0	-.00503	99
3202.4	180122.7	.01778	PRECISION
3929.6	197487.4	.01990	INSPECTOR
-19872.3	263665.5	-.07534	100
-6481.6	321683.6	-.02015	PLANT, SYSTEM
-337.7	334449.1	-.00101	OPERATORS
-14538.4	374207.7	-.03885	101
-4956.3	498191.3	-.00995	OTHER PRECS
2503.8	562896.5	.00445	PROD OPER
-52973.8	743095.1	-.07129	102
6163.9	908596.7	.00678	METAL, PLASTIC
-12896.8	838013.3	-.01539	MACH OP
-151814.3	1124893.0	-.13496	103
642.3	30491.1	.02106	FABRIC MACH
889.3	27971.4	.03179	OPER, NEC
-800.6	35059.6	-.02283	104
-26338.4	347594.4	-.07578	METAL, PLASTIC
-23356.7	328773.5	-.07104	MACH OPER
-84002.5	436278.2	-.19254	105
801.1	364288.2	.00212	PRINT MCH
1996.0	385945.8	.00517	OPER
-18195.2	445054.3	-.04088	106
-29997.3	341844.5	-.08775	TEXTILE MACH
-44720.3	331938.5	-.13472	OPER
-101293.8	405599.6	-.24974	107
-116070.8	877953.4	-.13221	TEXTILE SEW
-164714.7	897642.1	-.18350	MACH OPER

Table A3.1 (cont.)

NX	C	Ratio	Occupation
-296504.8	1040571.0	-.28494	108
-78.6	94398.0	-.00083	LAUND, DRY
28.3	107225.1	.00026	CLEAN OP
-1221.2	118743.9	-.01028	109
-365.0	303167.8	-.00120	PACK MACH
1255.3	312614.3	.00402	OPERATORS
-17836.1	358081.8	-.04981	110
-3314.3	50091.5	-.06617	FURNACE OP
-3468.2	46459.4	-.07465	KILN, OVEN
-11139.7	60006.4	-.18564	111
-34924.1	643884.1	-.05424	OTHER SPEC
-41877.5	646545.6	-.06477	MACH OP
-112104.0	761253.5	-.14726	112
16902.9	789751.3	-.02140	MISC MACH
-8605.6	801554.1	-.01074	OPER
-75122.1	964120.8	-.07792	113
-1530.3	352041.4	-.00435	WELDERS,
908.6	320079.3	.00284	CUTTERS
-35157.8	402963.2	-.08725	114
-2384.1	36947.6	-.06453	SOLDERERS
-3720.9	37163.5	-.10012	BRAZERS
-8934.8	45101.0	-.19811	115
-24365.0	988123.1	-.02466	
-38953.1	975631.4	-.03993	ASSEMBLERS
-208504.0	1349960.0	-.15445	116
-22311.8	537351.3	-.04152	HAND-WORK
-34355.6	537903.3	-.06387	OCCUPAT
-97006.1	645724.3	-.15023	117
-19162.6	374899.9	-.05111	OTHER PROD
-26074.7	370467.6	-.07038	INSPECTOR
-83809.6	478505.4	-.17515	119
43868.1	1699701.0	.02581	TRUCK
66569.7	1731480.0	.03845	DRIVERS
-1945.0	2052908.0	.00095	120
1671.1	649412.4	.00257	OTHER MOTOR
2620.0	667210.8	.00394	VEH OPER
-2461.5	717449.9	-.00343	122
23722.0	114520.6	.20714	RAIL, WATER
24546.4	112093.4	.21898	TRANS OCC
17347.8	134163.4	.12930	123
-8745.4	96214.2	-.09089	CRANE, HOIST
-4908.4	88635.7	-.05538	WINCH OP

Table A3.1 (cont.)

NX	C	Ratio	Occupation
-13025.8	111119.4	-.11722	125
-100.5	4830.9	-.02080	EXC, GRADER
255.3	4700.1	.05432	DOZER OP
-405.2	5669.0	-.07148	126
-35060.3	802161.0	-.04371	OTHER MAT
-13656.9	783824.5	-.01742	MOV EQU OP
-63823.8	936329.0	-.06816	127
-23336.4	443248.2	-.05265	HELPERS,
-9285.2	420525.2	-.02208	CRAFT, PROD
-15995.9	515203.8	-.03105	129
-23087.1	786511.0	-.02935	FREIGHT
-22118.9	796588.9	-.02777	MAT HAND
-89554.2	953887.4	-.09388	131
1538.1	326591.8	.00471	GAGE, SRV
1893.0	348537.2	.00543	STATION OCC
-2621.9	410697.0	-.00638	132
-10628.8	284677.9	-.03733	HAND PACK
-14623.1	286329.1	-.05107	PACKAGERS
-45481.9	335642.8	-.13551	133
2783.8	1874687.0	.00148	LABORERS,
16477.8	1911957.0	.008620	EXC CONSTR
-73819.8	2248051.0	-.03284	134

Table A3.2 Total Number of Job Losses, by Occupation, 1977-1982
and 1982-1985

1977-1982	1982-1985		
0.	0.	1	OCCUPATIONS 1-9
9.	-73.	2	EXECUTIVES/ADMINISTRATORS
120.	-712.	3	
50174.	-179294.	4	
9792.	-23321.	5	
2091.	-6990.	6	
2205.	-12059.	7	
255.	-746.	8	
1962.	-18416.	9	
625.	-1516.	10	OCCUPATIONS 10-29
1356.	-3256.	11	PROFESSIONALS
5033.	-24409.	12	
437.	-11912.	13	
591.	-17266.	14	
8998.	-23974.	15	
888.	-865.	16	
3681.	-9882.	17	
516.	-1095.	18	
1703.	-4955.	19	
8819.	-4501.	20	
206.	-759.	21	
557.	-1685.	22	
118.	-383.	23	
561.	-3973.	24	
686.	-935.	25	
421.	-1136.	26	
3166.	-6437.	27	
4343.	-19164.	28	
950.	-2742.	29	
390.	-1270.	30	OCCUPATIONS 30-39
29.	-2129.	31	TECHNICAL
5551.	-20060.	32	
210.	-7776.	33	
3145.	-19288.	34	
8277.	-21206.	35	
1800.	-3587.	36	
88.	-801.	37	
4391.	-12439.	38	
6531.	-14669.	39	
2520.	-2790.	40	OCCUPATIONS 40-43
3402.	-7388.	41	SALES

Table A3.2 (cont.)

1977-1982	1982-1985		
6083.	-11135.	42	
20386.	-93158.	43	
3341.	-8328.	44	OCCUPATIONS 44-62
20424.	-65525.	45	ADMINISTRATIVE SUPPORT
5642.	-18698.	46	
2362.	-5162.	47	
3458.	-6859.	48	
2186.	-4275.	49	
3693.	-16879.	50	
11790.	-41042.	51	
1068.	-7791.	52	
1789.	-9337.	53	
2656.	-7842.	54	
3851.	-18146.	55	
331.	-17786.	56	
1001.	-35808.	57	
6544.	-34964.	58	
1627.	-11545.	59	
1237.	-2515.	60	
1969.	-9750.	61	
30474.	-81672.	62	
173.	-451.	63	OCC 63 PERSONAL HOUSEHOLD
4956.	-20772.	64	OCCUPATIONS 64-65
-1.	-89.	65	PROTECTIVE SERVICES
20683.	-61121.	66	OCCUPATIONS 66-69
375.	-1498.	67	SERVICES
10770.	-49859.	68	
6203.	-19081.	69	
27176.	-63018.	70	OCC 70 FARMING
4157.	-10649.	71	OCCUPATIONS 71-91
791.	-33231.	72	PRECISION PRODUCT WORKERS
724.	-3931.	73	
448.	-2010.	74	
18394.	-90723.	75	
7237.	-104979.	76	
3464.	-8713.	77	
2906.	-19535.	78	
1487.	-3616.	79	
2861.	-9908.	80	
4455.	-9393.	81	
53431.	-9934.	82	
-4021.	-21039.	83	

Table A3.2 (cont.)

1977-1982	1982-1985		
-1386.	-36423.	84	
-323.	-11243.	85	
-7425.	-32169.	86	
-9397.	-23654.	87	
-157.	-2214.	88	
727.	-23802.	89	
6144.	-14201.	90	
7460.	-55478.	91	
-19061.	-138918.	92	OCCUPATIONS 92-107
247.	-1690.	93	MACHINE OPERATORS
2982.	-60646.	94	
1195.	-20191.	95	
-14723.	-56573.	96	
-48644.	-131790.	97	
107.	-1250.	98	
1620.	-19091.	99	
-154.	-7672.	100	
-6953.	-70227.	101	
8297.	-66516.	102	
2439.	-36066.	103	
-1337.	-5214.	104	
-14588.	-169551.	105	
-12044.	-62651.	106	
-6912.	-57735.	107	
22702.	-68515.	108	OCCUPATIONS 108-113
949.	-5082.	109	TRANSPORT OCCUPATIONS
824.	-7199.	110	
3837.	-8117.	111	
356.	-661.	112	
21403.	-50167.	113	
14051.	-6711.	114	OCCUPATIONS 114-118
968.	-67435.	115	HANDLERS
355.	-4515.	116	
-3994.	-30859.	117	
13694.	-90298.	118	

Table A3.3. Ratios of Earnings in Each Occupation to Earnings of
All Full-Time Workers for Each Education Category, 1980
(Occupation titles follow earnings data.)

1.28561	1.13422	1.24872	1.20483	1.19258
1.17582	1.07380	1.04566		

OFFICIALS + ADMINISTRATORS

1.28910	.90847	1.22517	1.03168	1.01123
.94191	.86744	.89142		

ADMINISTRATORS, EDUCATION

1.23137	1.13168	1.08746	1.06647	1.17689
1.16190	1.13037	1.02025		

OTHER SPECIFIED MANAGERS

1.45237	1.32736	1.46144	1.35401	1.32369
1.33432	1.35270	1.24351		

MANAGERS, NEC, SALARIED

1.23896	1.02138	1.33556	1.09277	1.02645
1.02910	1.03335	.96270		

ACCOUNTANTS AND AUDITORS

1.16550	1.08125	1.35653	1.24701	1.19643
1.08752	.96082	.90673		

PERSONNEL SPECIALISTS

1.09082	1.06219	1.24520	1.17044	1.13119
1.07399	.93702	.86386		

BUYERS + PURCHASING AGENTS

1.13136	1.10989	1.31516	1.26731	1.21787
1.11477	.93228	.83235		

INSPECTORS

1.34922	1.15042	1.61106	1.30545	1.14894
1.15694	1.13860	1.12768		

OTHER MANAGEMENT

1.52987	1.11606	1.83102	1.15718	1.43465
1.37633	1.16962	1.00720		

ARCHITECTS

1.55410	1.23443	1.63375	1.33620	1.39368
1.35124	1.23642	1.08659		

CIVIL ENGINEERS

1.56783	1.28003	1.69080	1.43053	1.55482
1.40556	1.22171	1.10126		

ELECTRICAL ENGINEERS

1.35220	1.20679	1.61399	1.36730	1.38374
1.28091	1.08614	.98211		

INDUSTRIAL ENGINEERS

1.56677	1.30879	1.76063	1.47800	1.55843
1.42232	1.24619	1.10108		

MECHANICAL ENGINEERS

Table A3.3.(cont.)

```
  1.64592   1.29320   2.06936    1.51383   1.53084
  1.40061   1.28873   1.14945
OTHER ENGINEERS
  1.08183   1.08180   1.20978    1.39062   1.12513
  1.10695    .87330    .81632
SURVEYORS
  1.42511   1.20178   1.76384    1.49043   1.46900
  1.33792   1.08884    .99928
SYSTEMS ANALYSTS
  1.46665   1.12567   1.52633    1.22661   1.19281
  1.10925   1.19388   1.05316
MATHEMATICIANS
  1.39283   1.03543   1.43152    1.16232   1.29592
  1.17639    .99471    .98386
CHEMISTS
  1.45047   1.04378   1.27800    1.03842   1.07083
  1.07100   1.02192   1.04469
OTHER NATURAL SCIENTISTS
  2.51482   1.60944   2.95040    2.01110   1.35990
  1.13335   1.47822   1.62370
HEALTH DIAGNOSING
   .93753    .85422    .98568     .90733    .98974
   .91198    .72651    .69582
REGISTERED NURSES
  1.02408    .79264    .92094     .75309    .75641
   .80603    .85123    .75878
OTHER HEALTH OCCUPATIONS
   .91498    .66400   1.00952     .82210    .82139
   .75845    .60846    .65228
TEACHERS
  1.44964   1.05549   1.43201    1.19278   1.26649
  1.24189   1.09764    .96970
SOCIAL SCIENTISTS
   .76319    .60055    .76114     .77503    .76705
   .69757    .60373    .50431
SOCIAL WORKERS
  2.14825   1.38844   1.83041    1.27956   1.23301
  1.32516   1.41415   1.39055
LAWYERS
  1.08236    .96087   1.13619    1.07383   1.08810
  1.03293    .87521    .78746
WRITERS + ARTISTS
   .97666    .68202    .85152     .81247    .79204
   .68307    .59453    .68192
```

Table A3.3.(cont.)

OTHER PROFESSIONAL OCCUPATIONS
```
.65192    .69962    .74280    .76255    .73439
.66032    .56597    .56568
```
LICENSED NURSES
```
.76294    .74580    .81671    .78614    .77253
.73827    .70253    .68948
```
OTHER HEALTH TECHNICIANS
```
1.09110   1.12885   1.24651   1.23803   1.21984
1.09103    .88580    .82583
```
ELECTRONIC TECHNICIANS
```
1.22247   1.19845   1.02370   1.30912   1.30404
1.19239   1.09808   1.02778
```
INDUSTRIAL TECHNICIANS
```
1.02214   1.03705   1.15324   1.16369   1.13610
1.02754    .80808    .70390
```
DRAFTING + SURVEYING TECH
```
1.09141   1.08033   1.20463   1.19448   1.19412
1.07185    .88707    .83274
```
OTHER SCIENCE, ENGINEERING TECH
```
1.91726   1.73733   1.69907   1.87413   1.96934
1.97554   1.50549   1.25092
```
AIRPLANE PILOTS
```
1.14758   1.17584   1.06475   1.01312   1.20833
1.25333   1.00544    .86190
```
CONTROLLERS
```
1.18142   1.03356   1.35176   1.30794   1.25976
1.10028    .92236    .84464
```
COMPUTER PROGRAMMERS
```
1.18205   1.07922   1.19660   1.16033   1.21906
1.16169    .95690    .84245
```
OTHER TECHNICIANS
```
1.32714   1.23284   1.37727   1.30213   1.28798
1.27592   1.17038   1.03881
```
SALES, FINANCE + SERVICES
```
.60659    .67746    .70705    .68347    .68341
.66486    .58422    .53306
```
CASHIERS
```
.73692    .78569    .79977    .77746    .78617
.81191    .75903    .65754
```
OTHER SALES, RETAIL, PERS SER
```
1.01717   1.04686   1.07179   1.01636   1.12308
1.04317    .91571    .81967
```
SALES RELATED OCCUPATIONS

Table A3.3.(cont.)

.83632	.86691	1.10158	.94163	.88569
.84885	.79776	.73397		

COMPUTER OPERATORS

.68718	.56550	.88118	.79213	.76853
.69654	.56520	.53347		

SECRETARIES

.65756	.71399	.86442	.77127	.72778
.68934	.55951	.50077		

STENO AND TYPISTS

.57357	.62260	.72770	.69108	.63867
.57897	.49312	.49815		

RECEPTIONISTS

.81981	.84110	.89351	.85165	.87576
.85003	.72338	.66455		

OTHER INFORMATION CLERKS

.68831	.74814	.87285	.81351	.74063
.72799	.68447	.64759		

FILE CLERKS

.74468	.79444	.90474	.86404	.81641
.76365	.65468	.62032		

OTHER RECORDS CLERKS

.70324	.74776	.88844	.81757	.76556
.70855	.67522	.62343		

ACCOUNTING CLERKS

.76475	.83154	1.05970	.90718	.85293
.77990	.65836	.53765		

PAYROLL CLERKS

.73763	.78101	.97128	.83697	.78490
.75883	.71603	.74354		

OTHER FINANCIAL CLERKS

.70217	.78014	.89416	.84749	.79234
.69926	.62288	.57383		

TELEPHONE OPERATORS

1.03965	1.13342	1.18683	1.22409	1.18355
1.06792	.81185	.66664		

POSTAL CLERKS, MAIL CARRIERS

.93797	.98207	1.10656	1.05625	1.01597
.95520	.81688	.81077		

PRODUCTION COORDINATORS

.79337	.89429	1.01221	.91777	.89746
.84434	.67717	.60289		

SHIPPING CLERKS

.80960	.89442	1.02851	.96778	.90250

Table A3.3.(cont.)

.83108 .72172 .62219
STOCK AND INVENTORY CLERKS
.85456 .95422 1.05559 .99914 .95364
.90038 .77625 .82935
RECORDING CLERKS
.88689 .86414 1.06410 .97077 .89854
.87663 .78156 .72688
INVESTIGATORS
.67638 .74065 .90267 .83657 .75573
.68261 .59265 .53251
DATA ENTRY KEYERS
.72194 .76119 .93668 .83009 .77074
.73062 .67870 .69898
OTHER ADMIN SUPPORT OCCUP
.32264 .38810 .40649 .39011 .37859
.34578 .37398 .24698
PRIVATE HOUSEHOLD OCCUP
.79659 .87021 .86281 .88776 .90799
.83773 .78195 .66061
GUARDS
1.00497 1.02594 1.06601 1.10192 1.07690
1.02731 .87114 .78473
OTHER PROTECTIVE SERVICES
.51399 .58902 .65023 .58987 .57971
.57378 .48979 .43177
FOOD SERVICE OCCUPATIONS
.56541 .62419 .67240 .63422 .62018
.60149 .53025 .74008
HEALTH SERVICE OCCUPATIONS
.68507 .80614 .82446 .79835 .81979
.77931 .62654 .51074
CLEANING SERVICE
.59495 .65390 .67700 .66174 .66396
.64318 .57434 .52846
PERSONAL SERVICES
.59979 .67237 .68937 .71170 .67684
.65239 .58863 .50996
FARM, FOREST AND FISH OCCUP
.82418 .94778 1.03251 .98579 .94380
.86249 .68364 .59589
AUTO MECHANICS
1.00424 1.15435 1.20206 1.17198 1.17336
1.06053 .83912 .72497

Table A3.3.(cont.)

INDUST MACHINERY REPAIRERS
.92918	1.01041	1.04284	1.02111	1.05559
.97437	.76094	.64436		

ELECTRONIC REPAIRERS
.98162	1.10232	1.20546	1.15547	1.11745
1.02710	.76776	.72361		

HEAT, AIR COND, REFRIG MECH
1.06690	1.19686	1.25674	1.22389	1.23526
1.11238	.83080	.70143		

OTHER MECH, REPAIR
1.05804	1.11520	1.11832	1.14188	1.15425
1.09839	1.00995	.92449		

SUPERVISORS, CONSTRUCT
.91279	1.03791	1.13299	1.09402	1.05625
.93461	.73862	.58491		

CARPENTERS
1.16439	1.29092	1.40071	1.34964	1.33279
1.19122	.95166	.79173		

ELECTRICIANS
.87993	1.02047	1.08928	1.06435	1.02847
.91160	.70942	.55340		

PAINTERS
1.12231	1.27575	1.32502	1.32671	1.30401
1.15436	.88841	.83171		

PLUMBERS
1.00547	1.15548	1.21692	1.15655	1.17734
1.07082	.84154	.68466		

OTHER CONSTRUCTION TRADES
1.15677	1.29783	1.45460	1.32063	1.28722
1.20635	1.16599	1.06661		

EXTRACTIVE OCCUPATIONS
1.17209	1.31385	1.46076	1.38204	1.33139
1.21176	.97486	.80616		

TOOL AND DIE MAKERS
.99796	1.13545	1.23743	1.18364	1.14460
1.03468	.78933	.67141		

MACHINISTS
1.07356	1.22371	1.34170	1.26349	1.23379
1.10801	.90991	.72503		

SHEET METAL WORKERS
1.02263	1.15994	1.25868	1.22858	1.17866
1.06034	.72030	.69235		

Table A3.3.(cont.)

OTHER PRECISION METAL
.63498	.74900	.84012	.75549	.72907
.64570	.52659	.46755		

PRECISION MACHINE WORKERS
.86372	.99936	1.04404	1.02619	1.00580
.92674	.67035	.56833		

PRECISION FOOD PROD
1.00624	1.11889	1.20110	1.14665	1.14802
1.06136	.83073	.66992		

PRECISION INSPECTORS
1.15589	1.25388	1.32493	1.33164	1.30136
1.15921	1.04067	.96945		

PLANT / SYSTEM OPERATORS
.81016	.91215	.99356	.93225	.91685
.88992	.67584	.62062		

OTHER PRECISION PROD OCCUP
.93511	1.08993	1.16964	1.11279	1.08422
.98956	.76030	.65348		

METAL AND PLASTIC MACH OPER
.85547	.99977	1.08654	1.01460	.99541
.88484	.60415	.56520		

FABRICATING MACH OPER, NEC
.81346	.95363	.99372	.96334	.95444
.90059	.66365	.54645		

METAL,PLASTIC PROCESS MACH
.94203	1.05431	1.16686	1.13336	1.08693
.93651	.66870	.57269		

PRINTING MACHINE OPERATORS
.61277	.74170	.81032	.72528	.71369
.67352	.60703	.41292		

TEXTILE MACHINE OPERATORS
.49543	.60018	.64727	.60610	.56981
.53444	.43130	.39040		

TEXTILE SEWING MACHINE OPER
.55786	.66159	.68650	.65160	.65278
.68559	.61154	.41889		

LAUNDRY/DRYCLEAN MACH OP
.79622	.93029	.99341	.90653	.93089
.91451	.72051	.59444		

PACKAGING MACHINE OPERS
1.06493	1.23486	1.29884	1.26463	1.24848
1.10446	.87201	.70462		

FURNACE, KILN, OVEN OPER

Table A3.3.(cont.)

.85145	.98571	.99447	.98221	1.00697
.94834	.75225	.65658		

OTHER SPECIF MACH OPER

.83028	.96839	.99616	.96079	.97961
.92723	.75372	.64243		

MISCELLANEOUS MACH OPER

.97062	1.12940	1.23840	1.15199	1.11618
1.03708	.79450	.66082		

WELDERS AND CUTTERS

.63311	.74661	.81648	.75491	.73597
.64612	.56255	.41236		

SOLDERERS AND BRAZERS

.77254	.89833	.94180	.90521	.90160
.84475	.65792	.51196		

ASSEMBLERS

.78527	.90591	.96889	.92545	.93584
.82114	.56293	.39056		

HAND-WORKING OCCUPATIONS

.85302	.97021	.96282	.95551	.99336
.97258	.78334	.68656		

OTHER PRODUCTION

.93571	1.09258	1.17669	1.13990	1.07898
.96655	.76101	.62180		

TRUCK DRIVERS

.80809	.91419	.96514	.95667	.94287
.83598	.65466	.53355		

OTHER MOTOR VEH OPERS

1.23639	1.38348	1.50887	1.48933	1.41119
1.25450	1.01941	.82320		

RAIL,WATER TRANSPORT

1.13370	1.33802	1.46228	1.35729	1.31596
1.16852	.87253	.78844		

CRANE, HOIST,WINCH OPER

.94381	1.12200	1.17471	1.12114	1.11990
1.00132	.91123	.65839		

EXCAVATING,GRADING,DOZER

.91710	1.07360	1.15460	1.09754	1.06147
.96943	.79496	.67323		

OTHER MAT MOVING EQUIP OPER

.78438	.91457	.98829	.90478	.91775
.83024	.66781	.64782		

HELPERS, CRAFT, PRODUCTION

.82111	.94493	.99634	.95782	.94946

Table A3.3.(cont.)

```
.90452    .69692    .58719
FREIGHT, STOCK, MATERIAL HAND
 .63155    .73582    .79151    .71953    .73335
 .70445    .65976    .50657
GARAGE, SERVICE STATION
 .67748    .80148    .83242    .80576    .79691
 .76915    .56403    .50104
HAND PACKERS AND PACKAGERS
 .83494    .95973    .99935    .98160    .96528
 .90699    .78575    .62826
LABORERS, EXC CONSTRUCTION
```

Table A3.4. Ratios of Earnings for Men in Each Occupation to
Earnings of All Full-Time Male Workers for Each
Education Category, 1980

```
1.22272  1.07850  1.15708  1.12264  1.16137
1.12552  1.01360  1.00180  1   1
1.24739   .89162  1.23577  1.07504  1.12402
 .99183   .89723   .86210  3   4
1.20544  1.09777  1.08888  1.10160  1.17967
1.11203  1.07583   .99072  2   6
1.40767  1.29949  1.45203  1.35065  1.29504
1.28821  1.32172  1.23575  5  708
1.24855  1.00554  1.43089  1.24675  1.17363
1.05484   .98838   .93451  6   9
1.17654  1.08251  1.32846  1.25830  1.22324
1.09568   .97408   .91680  7  10
1.06829  1.03487  1.21955  1.16234  1.12396
1.04095   .91631   .84380  3  11
1.01904  1.00884  1.23286  1.16499  1.09166
1.00512   .85720   .78550  4  12
1.40787  1.17041  1.66555  1.48101  1.34859
1.20707  1.10448  1.09941  5  13
1.36702  1.02945  1.73659  1.04618  1.28068
1.23687  1.07775   .94299  8  14
1.36818  1.11015  1.51382  1.18615  1.22063
1.19603  1.11081  1.00462  9  15
1.38676  1.14925  1.56911  1.32756  1.37206
1.24737  1.10009  1.01926  10  16
1.21951  1.09551  1.51870  1.34055  1.26762
1.15169   .98660   .91448  11  17
1.37631  1.16983  1.60650  1.32035  1.35770
1.25438  1.11886  1.01695  12  18
1.45295  1.16716  1.90150  1.36835  1.35080
1.24024  1.16179  1.06387  6  19
 .95354   .95944  1.10894  1.23665   .98433
 .97900   .78910   .75886  13  20
1.30546  1.10653  1.80488  1.50361  1.40078
1.22987  1.00804   .93606  14  21
1.48436  1.12320  1.66892  1.34676  1.33955
1.18236  1.20082  1.02754  7  23
1.27410   .97042  1.46179  1.08514  1.19843
1.07585   .93119   .93606  16  24
1.33848   .98957  1.23729   .92758   .99401
 .99967   .96299   .99992  8  25
2.29268  1.53887  2.76423  1.95238  1.57441
1.32439  1.39946  1.54391  17  26
```

Table A3.4. (cont.)

.98374	.83999	1.08130	.80375	.90470
.88331	.73995	.83436	18 27	
1.02637	.78731	1.04417	.79847	.77210
.76664	.86321	.74926	9 28	
.90012	.67124	1.07317	.95382	.93211
.80747	.60143	.64561	19 29	
1.41115	1.04901	1.56585	1.24242	1.40601
1.28471	1.10009	.95763	20 30	
.65505	.51600	.68943	.72006	.67885
.60910	.54066	.44222	21 31	
1.96748	1.32959	2.25854	1.41126	1.38381
1.42824	1.36193	1.32357	22 32	
1.06039	.95401	1.16423	1.11544	1.08877
1.00117	.87757	.79276	23 33	
.87780	.63231	.75403	.75274	.72123
.60741	.53643	.63876	10 34	
.67828	.69539	.83089	.72439	.74804
.64061	.56568	.87982	24 35	
.83275	.76853	.93659	.83694	.82768
.78063	.68097	.71803	25 36	
.98258	1.01572	1.22602	1.17460	1.09922
.97433	.80786	.77889	26 37	
1.10971	1.08995	.94710	1.23709	1.18532
1.08126	.99682	.95456	11 38	
.92092	.93761	1.05892	1.05850	1.01927
.92568	.75175	.66590	12 39	
1.02561	1.01754	1.17703	1.18648	1.11899
.99456	.85399	.81428	13 40	
1.68757	1.54529	1.57073	1.68398	1.72063
1.74796	1.35031	1.15871	27 41	
1.16396	1.18741	1.07110	1.07025	1.27396
1.22791	.96788	.83889	14 42	
1.09408	.96499	1.31707	1.26263	1.21149
1.01867	.85791	.80971	28 43	
1.13589	1.04444	1.17236	1.15729	1.20366
1.10969	.93119	.82435	29 44	
1.32636	1.20468	1.49268	1.31169	1.30679
1.23221	1.14388	1.04006	31 47	
.68177	.73501	.72683	.73882	.76371
.73162	.62466	.59091	33 49	
.78978	.82571	.86341	.87013	.84856
.81797	.74888	.65948	34 50	
1.00232	1.03580	1.04228	.99134	1.10966
1.06534	.91689	.78428	35 51	

Table A3.4. (cont.)

.88386	.88896	1.17398	1.04906	.95431
.85064	.80340	.73652	37 53	
1.03020	.98034	1.13496	1.09812	.96214
.97550	.99643	.91294	38 54	
.92165	.94440	.94380	.94395	1.00312
.98523	.75626	.57474	15 55	
.73519	.73150	.82602	.85281	.78329
.66978	.70867	.62173	39 56	
.91310	.90980	1.00935	1.00758	1.02284
.89576	.75024	.67674	16 57	
.81649	.85451	1.02276	.94661	.89948
.80513	.70867	.67874	40 58	
.82927	.86504	.97561	.94949	.92167
.82147	.70956	.68259	41 59	
.87805	.84688	.96748	.95094	.92950
.82030	.78463	.70493	42 60	
.88386	.93238	1.22602	1.09812	1.00653
.85764	.71135	.57627	43 61	
.93635	.92928	1.12501	1.01892	1.00259
.90565	.80054	.78476	17 62	
.82695	.87144	.92683	1.04329	.91906
.78530	.78374	.72804	44 63	
.94657	1.03014	1.12520	1.13564	1.07311
.96616	.74888	.63020	45 64	
.95032	.98374	1.13828	1.09444	1.04401
.93533	.80237	.81021	18 65	
.73287	.82965	.96423	.86003	.82768
.77013	.62824	.57242	46 66	
.77468	.85651	.99837	.94517	.86423
.78296	.69080	.60786	47 67	
.82700	.92420	1.06041	1.01042	.91598
.84508	.74819	.81831	19 68	
.96400	.89520	1.10894	1.08947	1.03655
.93349	.77212	.72111	48 69	
.82230	.85374	1.11382	1.01443	.93342
.77713	.70688	.59245	49 70	
.87706	.87756	1.01440	.97074	.93296
.84575	.76665	.76161	20 71	
.44483	.51157	.52033	.48052	.47781
.54376	.88740	.36364	50 72	
.71312	.78480	.79512	.80664	.81071
.75263	.71314	.61864	51 73	
.88720	.90904	.98194	.98944	.94272

.90873	.78933	.73165	21 74	
.53194	.60748	.67480	.62338	.60444
.57410	.47989	.42373	52 75	
.65041	.66299	.77073	.68110	.65144
.60443	.55228	.84900	53 76	
.65389	.77300	.82276	.78211	.76893
.71529	.58624	.49076	54 77	
.66899	.73515	.78049	.76623	.76110
.69428	.61126	.56626	55 78	
.54123	.61324	.64228	.64935	.60705
.59510	.54424	.48844	56 79	
.72228	.83505	.94361	.87290	.81988
.75943	.61282	.55070	22 81	
.88502	1.02238	1.10407	1.04618	1.02480
.93699	.75424	.67180	58 82	
.81998	.89193	.96098	.91198	.92298
.86114	.68901	.60709	59 83	
.86063	.96870	1.10406	1.02309	.97128
.90432	.68633	.66641	60 84	
.94201	1.05967	1.15750	1.09438	1.08096
.98547	.75315	.65140	12 85	
1.18831	1.28292	1.42228	1.37287	1.32152
1.21678	1.08715	.93480	23 86	
.80139	.91707	1.03740	.97114	.91906
.82380	.66309	.54237	61 87	
1.02439	1.13654	1.28780	1.20491	1.16188
1.05018	.85523	.73421	62 88	
.77933	.91238	1.00488	.95094	.90339
.81214	.64969	.52003	63 89	
.98490	1.12334	1.21138	1.17605	1.13446
1.01867	.79714	.76656	64 90	
.88349	1.02083	1.11438	1.02693	1.02586
.94512	.75286	.63674	10 91	
1.01626	1.14966	1.33008	1.17172	1.12141
1.06651	1.04915	.98998	65 92	
1.03020	1.15604	1.34472	1.23232	1.15927
1.06651	.87578	.74884	67 94	
.88386	1.00783	1.15285	1.06638	1.00261
.91482	.71224	.62635	68 95	
.94890	1.08440	1.23740	1.12987	1.08094
.98133	.82127	.67257	69 96	
.93929	1.06901	1.22772	1.15569	1.06768
.96366	.68488	.67242	24 97	

.64692	.77235	.88130	.77201	.74282
.65694	.56658	.53467	70	98
.79791	.92690	1.00813	.96825	.91906
.84597	.62198	.54854	71	99
.96748	1.06963	1.29756	1.16595	1.09791
.96849	.77659	.64176	72	100
1.01974	1.11081	1.21789	1.18759	1.13838
1.02567	.94191	.90139	73	101
.79111	.88919	1.00476	.92514	.89448
.85118	.63512	.60449	25	102
.86063	1.00763	1.12683	1.05195	.98564
.89382	.69616	.61556	74	103
.83508	.98055	1.09756	1.03752	.96475
.81330	.56211	.52928	75	104
.75511	.89143	.94747	.91251	.88366
.82315	.60477	.52238	26	105
.89199	.99920	1.15935	1.09957	1.01828
.88331	.65058	.55932	76	106
.60835	.74355	.82028	.72473	.70794
.66935	.64827	.49393	27	107
.59814	.72790	.75285	.74603	.71018
.66394	.63539	.53698	77	108
.60395	.70439	.78049	.71573	.69321
.65228	.57819	.42142	78	109
.80139	.93474	1.04065	.92929	.92689
.87281	.69080	.62943	79	110
.94077	1.09812	1.20163	1.13276	1.09138
.97783	.78195	.65794	80	111
.81893	.95190	1.01567	.97100	.95359
.87968	.70935	.63401	28	112
.80139	.93750	1.00488	.95238	.93342
.86114	.71314	.62943	81	113
.86179	1.00875	1.14797	1.03752	.98172
.91949	.71671	.61402	82	114
.70616	.83171	.86829	.83550	.85509
.71879	.53172	.50616	83	115
.78165	.90840	.98699	.94661	.90601
.81330	.63986	.50462	84	116
.76344	.88464	.98232	.92779	.89713
.77348	.58468	.39942	1	117
.90708	1.01838	1.13008	1.09091	1.03394
.93466	.74888	.67797	86	119
.82338	.96920	1.07769	1.01339	.94187

Table A3.4. (cont.)

.85562	.68494	.57633	2 120	
.73237	.83369	.89564	.88005	.85352
.75992	.59320	.50173	11 122	
1.08547	1.21856	1.38045	1.32283	1.22757
1.10713	.91469	.76292	3 123	
.99541	1.18601	1.33817	1.20255	1.14710
1.02999	.78227	.73068	4 125	
.82795	.99577	1.07460	.99322	.97398
.88523	.82236	.60700	5 126	
.81570	.96302	1.06941	.98802	.93703
.86226	.71938	.62980	6 127	
.69969	.82243	.91967	.81235	.81245
.74236	.61189	.62826	7 129	
.74816	.86558	.94142	.88196	.86189
.81824	.64122	.55248	8 131	
.56166	.65979	.73389	.64541	.64641
.63050	.59632	.46632	9 132	
.68757	.81270	.87154	.80952	.80809
.76663	.55228	.52542	91 133	
.72242	.84679	.91382	.86003	.83943
.78063	.64701	.57550	92 134	

Bibliography

Aho, C. Micheal and James Orr. "Trade-Sensitive Employment: Who are the Affected Workers?" *Monthly Labor Review* 104 (February 1981): 29-35.

Akerlof, George. "Gift Exchange and Efficiency Wages: Four Views." *American Economic Review* 74 (May 1984): 79-83.

Balassa, Bela. "A Stages Approach to Comparative Advantage." World Bank Reprint Series 136. Washington, D.C., 1977.

Baldwin, Robert. "Determinants of the Commodity Structure of U.S. Trade." *American Economic Review* 61 (March 1971): 126-146.

Bartel, Ann P. and Frank Lichtenberg. "Technical Change, Learning, and Wages." National Bureau of Economic Research Working Paper 2732, October 1988.

Bluestone, Barry and Bennett Harrison. *The Deindustrialization of America.* New York: Basic Books, 1982.

Bowen, Harry P. "On the Theoretical Interpretations of Indices of Trade Intensity and Revealed Comparative Advantage." *Weltwirtschaftliches Archiv* 119 (September 1983): 464-472.

Bowen, Harry P., Edward E. Leamer, and Leo Sveikauskas. "Multifactor Multicountry Tests of the Factor Abundance Hypothesis." *American Economic Review* 77 (December 1987):791-809.

Branson, William F., and Nicholas Monoyios. "Factor Inputs in U.S. Trade." *Journal of International Economics* 7 (May 1977): 111-131.

Clague, Christopher. "Information Costs, Corporate Hierarchies, and Earnings Inequality." *American Economic Review* 67 (February 1977): 81-85.

Dickens, William J., and Lawrence F. Katz. "Interindustry Wage Differences and Theories of Wage Determination." National Bureau of Economic Research Working Paper 2271, June 1987.

Fain, Scott. "Self-Employed Americans: Their Numbers Have Increased." *Monthly Labor Review* 103 (November 1980): 3-8.

Freeman, Richard B. "The Exit Voice Tradeoff in the Labor Market, Unionism, Job Tenure, Quits, and Separations." *Quarterly Journal of Economics* 94 (June 1980): 643-673.

Grinols, Earl L., and Steven J. Matusz. "Some Welfare Implications of Job Mobility in General Equilibrium." *American Economic Review* 78 (March 1988): 261-266.

Harkness, Jon. "Factor Abundance and Comparative Advantage." *American Economic Review* 68 (December 1978): 784-800.

Harkness, Jon, and John F. Kyle. "Factors Influencing United States Comparative Advantage." *Journal of International Economics* 5 (May 1975): 153-165.

Katz, Lawrence F., and Lawrence H. Summers. "Can Interindustry Wage Differentials Justify Strategic Trade Policy?" National Bureau of Economic Research Working Paper 2739, October 1988.

Keesing, Donald. "Labor Skills and International Trade: Evaluating Many Trade Flows With a Single Measuring Device." *Review of Economics and Statistics* 41 (May 1965): 287-294.

Keesing, Donald. "The Impact of Research and Development on United States Trade." *Journal of Political Economy* 75 (February 1967): 38-48.

Kenen, Peter B. "Nature, Capital, and Trade." *Journal of Political Economy* 73 (October 1965): 437-459.

Krueger, Alan B., and Lawrence H. Summers. "Efficiency Wages and the Interindustry Wage Structure." *Econometrica* 56 (March 1988):259-272.

Kreinen, Mordechai. "Comparative Labor Effectiveness and the Leontieff Scarce Factor Paradox." *American Economic Review* 55 (March 1965): 131-139.

Kutcher, Ronald, and Valerie Personick. "Deindustrialization and the Shift to Services." *Monthly Labor Review* 109 (June 1986): 3-13.

Lane, Julia. "An Empirical Estimate of the Effects of Labor Market Distortions on the Factor Content of U.S. Trade." *Journal of International Economics* 18 (May 1985): 187-193.

Lawrence, Robert Z. "Sectoral Shifts and the Size of the Middle Class." *Brookings Review* 3 (Fall 1985): 3-10.

Leamer, Edward E. "The Leontieff Paradox Reconsidered." *Journal of Political Economy* 88 (June 1980): 253-266.

Leamer, Edward E., and Harry P. Bowen. "Cross-Section Tests of the Heckscher-Ohlin Theorem: Comment." *American Economic Review* 71 (December 1981): 1040-1043.

Leontieff, Wassily. "Domestic Production and Foreign Trade: The American Capital Position Reexamined." *Econ. Internazionale* 7 (February 1954): 3-32.

Leontieff, Wassily. "Factor Proportions and the Structure of American Trade: Further Theoretical and Empirical Analysis." *Review of Economics and Statistics* 24 (November 1956): 386-407.

Maskus, Keith E. "A Test of the Heckscher-Ohlin-Vanek Theorem: The Leonteiff Commomplace." *Journal of International Economics* 19 (August 1986): 201-212.

Maskus, Keith, Catherine Sveikauskas, and Allan Webster. "The Composition of the Human Capital Stock and Its Relation to International Trade: Evidence from the U.S. and Britain" *Weltwirtschaftliches Archiv* 130 (March 1994): 50-76.

McMahon, Patrick, and John Tschetter. "The Declining Middle Class: A Further Analysis." *Monthly Labor Review* 109 (September 1986): 22-27.

Mincer, Jacob. *Schooling, Experience, and Earnings*. New York: Columbia University Press, 1974.

Pencavel, John. *An Analysis of the Quit Rate in American Manufacturing Industry*. Princeton: Princeton Industrial Relations Section, 1970.

Rosenthal, Neal H. "The Shrinking Middle Class: Myth or Reality?" *Monthly Labor Review* 108 (March 1985): 3-10.

Rousslang, Donald, and Steven Parker. *U.S. Trade-Related Employment: 1974-84*. U.S. International Trade Commission Publication Number 1855. Washington, D.C.: Government Printing Office, 1986.

Schoeple, Gregory. "Imports and Domestic Employment: Identifying Affected Industries." *Monthly Labor Review* 105 (August 1982): 13-26.

Stone, Charles, and Isabel Sawhill. "Labor Market Implications of the Growing Internationalization of the U.S. Economy." National Commission on Employment Policy Research Report 86-20. Washington, D.C., June 1988.

Sveikauskas, Leo. "Science and Technology in United States Foreign Trade." *Economic Journal* 103 (September 1983): 542-554.

Taubman, Paul. *Sources of Inequality in Earnings*. New York: North-Holland Publishing Company, 1975.

Taubman, Paul, and Terence Wales. "Higher Education, Mental Ability, and Screening." *Journal of Political Economy* 81 (January 1973): 28-55.

Thurow, Lester. "The Hidden Sting of the Trade Deficit." *The New York Times*. January 19, 1996, D-3.

U.S. Department of Commerce, Bureau of the Census. *1980 Census of Population Earnings by Occupation and Education*, Subject Report 8B. Washington, D.C.: Government Printing Office, May 1984.

Ulman, Lloyd. "Labor Mobility and the Interindustry Wage Structure in the Postwar United States." *Quarterly Journal of Economics* 79 (February 1965): 73-97.

Webster, Allan, "The Skill and Higher Educational Content of UK Net Exports." *Oxford Bulletin of Economics and Statistics* 55 (Fall 1993): 141-160.

Index